First Things First

God's Ways as a Lifestyle: Passion

Deborah F. Jenks

First Things First
by Deborah F. Jenks

Printed in the United States of America

Library of Congress Control Number: 2002107771
ISBN 1-591600-81-2

Unless otherwise indicated, Bible quotations are taken from the New King James Version Spirit-Filled Life Bible, © 1991 and the Holy Bible, NKJV, © 1982 by Thomas Nelson, Inc.

Xulon Press
11350 Random Hills Road
Suite 800
Fairfax, VA 22030
(703) 279-6511
XulonPress.com

To order additional copies, call 1-866-909-BOOK (2665).

To Chelsea,
Continue to
Dig deep into
the deep things
of God.
Blessings!
Deborah

To those who want to dive into
the deep things of God,
to love the Lord our God
with all our heart, soul, mind, and strength.

Endorsement

As Sovereign Love orchestrates the climax of human history, the church of Jesus Christ is being fashioned for her end time forerunner role by a radical shaking of priorities. God is calling us back to first things first—to the rediscovery of the first commandment and the recovery of our first love! All of heaven is trumpeting the invitation with climactic urgency to enter the sanctity and joy of holy, fiery love that the Father, Son and Spirit have known from eternity.

But the secret journey plotted by divine wisdom to bring us into that place of perfect love is along wilderness paths and into places of emptiness and desperation—the very paths and places where God appoints that our faith and love will grow most rapidly and bear witness to each other's strength and authenticity, as they are bolstered by a deepening hope in God that knows no disappointment.

By referencing her own personal journey into a fiery passion for the fullness of God, Deborah Jenks has shown the way into fresh places of worship, simplicity and joy that altogether satisfy the longings of the human heart and leave it at rest-focused, fulfilled and freed from those stifling spirits of religion that falsely bifurcate life into the sacred and the secular. She makes the pursuit of passion every believer's enterprise! Using her own experience of the goodness of God, she deftly crafts a portrait of the journey that takes us from glory to glory, while describing with clarity and understanding what happens to our hearts along the way.

As you read, you will see unfolded before you the manifold wisdom of God—the things He values, the virtues He inculcates, the pursuits He encourages, and the disciplines He appoints—all synergistically arranged to fashion in you the unique and glorious expression of the likeness of Jesus that heaven has envisioned in your calling and destiny.

First Things First will call you into deeper love, greater holiness, more zealous prayer, and unbridled celebration as you consider the ways of the Bridegroom-King who summons us to come away with Him.

Steve Carpenter
Director
Forerunner School of Prayer
Kansas City, Missouri

Acknowledgements

I am grateful to those who have gone before me in this experience and have provided resources to draw from. I am especially grateful to Mike Bickle. Although I have never personally met him, his teachings in the Friends of the Bridegroom Conferences and tapes have been a particular encouragement through these times. It has also been great to see the change in him as he has embraced his own teachings. Although this book is not about the Song of Solomon, it is greatly influenced by what I have learned in the Song of Solomon.

I am also deeply grateful to my family and friends who have walked with me through the good and hard times. I could not have made it without your encouragement and giving me permission to be "real" in what I was feeling.

Most of all, I am grateful to my God who is my husband and best friend.

> *I will stand my watch*
> *And set myself on the rampart,*
> *And watch to see what He will say to me,*
> *And what I will answer when I am corrected.*
> *Then the LORD answered me and said:*
> *"Write the vision*
> *And make it plain on tablets,*
> *That he may run who reads it.*
> *For the vision is yet for an appointed time;*
> *But at the end it will speak, and it will not lie.*
> *Though it tarries, wait for it;*
> *Because it will surely come,*
> *It will not tarry."* (Habakkuk 2:1–3)

Table of Contents

Introduction

T he purpose of this book is to invite you to the secret place with
God so that your passion for Him will be stirred. I have
touched on many areas in the book. As I prayed and researched
each section, my desire was to dive deeply into each one. Instead, I
have tried to create a menu to whet your appetite to know Him even
more, especially if you are in trying circumstances. The more I get
into this subject, the more I realize how little I know. It makes me
hungry to know God and His ways more and more. I hope it will do
the same for you.

The truth is that I was going to write a book titled *God's Ways in
Business*. But as I began writing, the first chapter became this book.
I knew the right foundation needed to be established for the other
books to follow. This book is born out of that need. I know that the
book on business (and others) will be written, but God said *First
Things First*.

This book is the fruit of a season with God in the wilderness
experience. While they have been tough years, they have also been
filled with wonderful times with God. Some of those times have
been in the secret place, some have been in corporate prayer meet-
ings, and others have been while reading a book or listening to a
tape and thinking, "Wow, that's what I am experiencing, too!" I feel
it is the culmination of the many different streams of life that God
has walked me through. The name He gave me for my ministry is
"Walking in His Ways." Because He has shown me how to walk (or
crawl in some cases), I want to help lead others to the right path.
Although we each have a deeply personal and unique walk, the

principles are similar. My heart is for this book to be an encouragement and practical guide to those who are radically walking in the wilderness to allow God to deal with their hearts.

God is the Same Yesterday, Today, and Forever

God's name, Jehovah (often translated as "Lord" or "I am"), means "I was that I was, I am that I am, and I will be what I will be." Hebrews 13:8 declares, *"Jesus Christ is the same yesterday, today, and forever."* Jesus hasn't changed since before the foundation of the world, or since the crucifixion, and His essence won't change after the second coming. His purposes have never changed since creation. Our understanding of God's purposes has definitely changed over time. Unfortunately, we humans don't have omniscience to know all things or omnipresence to be in all places at once. We have had a progressive understanding of who God is and His ways. *"Many people shall come and say, 'Come, and let us go up to the mountain of the LORD, To the house of the God of Jacob; He will teach us His ways, and we shall walk in His paths.' For out of Zion shall go forth the law, And the word of the LORD from Jerusalem"* (Isaiah 2:3). God wants to teach us His ways. But even more, He desires that we would **want** to know His ways **and** walk in them. He teaches us His ways by walking with us through all the circumstances of our lives, much like the poem "Footprints in the Sand."

God has revealed all things according to His timetable. He wants us to search Him out and His ways. It is a treasure hunt. He has hidden treasures with little corners sticking out of the earth. So if we take time, we will see the revealed corner, then begin to clear away the rocks and dirt to find the gem of wisdom. *"You have heard; See all this. And will you not declare it? I have made you hear new things from this time, Even hidden things, and you did not know them. They are created now and not from the beginning; And before this day you have not heard them, Lest you should say, 'Of course I knew them.' Surely you did not hear, surely you did not know; Surely from long ago your ear was not opened"* (Isaiah 48:6–8).

God did not reveal all truth at any one time. He unfolded His plan and purposes through successive writers, much in the same way that He doesn't reveal the whole plan for my life or yours all at once. "The principle of progressive revelation leads us to the principle of biblical continuity. By this we mean that the message of the Bible is the same unified message from Genesis to Revelation. The doctrines established in the Tanakh (Old Testament) are expanded in the Brit Hadasha (New Testament). Moreover, by the term 'biblical continuity' we are establishing the principle of consistency throughout all the scriptures." [1] God's message has never changed, only the messengers and form of the message.

In Genesis chapter 1, we see God speaking the world into existence out of chaos and nothingness. *"In the beginning **God created the heavens and the earth**. **The earth was without form, and void;** and darkness was on the face of the deep. And the **Spirit of God was hovering over the face of the waters**. Then **God said**, 'Let there be light'; and there was light. And God saw the light, that it was good; and God divided the light from the darkness"* (Genesis 1:1–4, emphasis added). We see references to all three persons of the Trinity, but in a hidden way. God the Father is clearly seen. Genesis 1:3 refers specifically to the Spirit of God. The spoken word (God said) or the third person is not explicit.

Genesis 1:26–27 states, *"Then God said, '**Let Us** make man in **Our image, according to Our likeness;** let them have dominion over the fish of the sea, over the birds of the air, and over the cattle, over all the earth and over every creeping thing that creeps on the earth.' So **God created man in His own image; in the image of God He created him; male and female** He created them"* (emphasis added). God created men and women in the image of God. What is interesting is that God speaks about Himself in the plural. The cry of Israel has always been, *"Hear, O Israel: **The LORD our God, the LORD is one!** You shall love the LORD your God with all your heart, with all your soul, and with all your strength"* (Deuteronomy 6:4–5, emphasis added). Is this a mistake, or is this a mystery?

It isn't until the Gospel of John that we understand that the word that was spoken at creation was and is Jesus, or *Yeshua* in Hebrew:

> *In the beginning was the **Word**, and the **Word was with God**, and the **Word was God**. He was in the beginning with God. **All things were made through Him**, and without Him nothing was made that was made. In Him was life, and the life was the light of men. And the light shines*

*in the darkness, and the darkness did not comprehend it. And **the Word became flesh and dwelt among us**, and we beheld His glory, the glory as of the only begotten of the Father, full of grace and truth. John bore witness of Him and cried out, saying, "This was He of whom I said, 'He who comes after me is preferred before me, for He was before me.'" And of His fullness we have all received, and grace for grace. For the law was given through Moses, but grace and truth came through Jesus Christ. No one has seen God at any time. **The only begotten Son, who is in the bosom of the Father, He has declared Him**.* (John 1:1–5, 14–18, emphasis added)

In the beginning, God (*Elohim*—a plural name for God) spoke the word (*Yeshua*) at creation while the Holy Spirit hovered over creation. Genesis 1:1–4 is a hidden example of the Trinity, but the full revelation (unveiling) did not come until after *Yeshua* brought the revelation. This is an example of progressive revelation.

New Wineskins

While God's message has never changed, sometimes the messenger and container of the message need to change.

*Then they said to Him, "Why do the disciples of John fast often and make prayers, and likewise those of the Pharisees, but Yours eat and drink?" And He said to them, "Can you make the **friends of the bridegroom** fast while the bridegroom is with them? But the days will come when the bridegroom will be taken away from them; then they will fast in those days." Then He spoke a parable to them: "No one puts **a piece from a new garment on an old one**; otherwise the new makes a tear, and also the piece that was taken out of the new does not match the old. And **no one puts new wine into old wineskins; or else the new wine will burst the wineskins and be spilled, and the wineskins will be ruined. But new wine must be put into new wineskins, and both are preserved.** And no one, having drunk old wine, immediately desires new; for he* *says, 'The old is better.'"* (Luke 5:33–39, emphasis added)

The Pharisees were asking Jesus why His disciples acted differently from the Pharisees (one extreme) and from John the Baptist's disciples (another extreme). I am sure His answer puzzled them! He said that His disciples were friends of the bridegroom and were with the bridegroom (Jesus). Then He talked about not putting a "new" fabric patch on an old garment. Finally, He used the illustration of not putting new wine into old wineskins. Not exactly a straight answer! He was actually pointing to the fact that spiritual life, as the Pharisees knew it, was changing! But it was changing at different rates for different groups.

Jesus did not say the old wine (or wineskin) was bad. In fact, He pointed out that most people prefer aged wine, as it is more palatable. While I was living in England, a big splash was made each year when a fresh batch of Beaujolais Nouveau landed in the stores from France. I tried some, and it tasted raw and bitter. Aged wine from a good year is definitely better than the new wine, in my opinion! Yet the mellowed wine would never exist without first passing through the stage of new wine. There is a process where the new things must become visible, tempered, and finally palatable.

The primary message Jesus communicated was that the old holder of spirituality cannot contain the new wave of God without first being renewed. For example, an old wineskin is very useful and serviceable for old wine. It is the best container for the job! But it is not the best container for new wine. A wineskin is an animal skin that is filled with new wine and sewn shut while the wine ferments. The chemical reactions from fermentation cause the skin to stretch to its limits from the escaping gases. As the wine ages, the force of the reactions ceases and comes to quiescence. Through the process, the wineskin becomes hardened in the new shape. It is not flexible as it was originally. If it is not retreated, it will burst when it is filled with new wine, thus spilling the new wine and ruining the old wineskin. This does not mean the new wine is not good or that the old wineskin is not of use. They just should not be used together.

The old wineskin can remain in service for the old wine, be thrown away, or be renewed. God has a definite purpose in His kingdom for some of the old wineskins—the current institutions and people of the church. They have served God and His people faithfully for the long term. They are often most palatable to the majority of people. The old wineskins must remain in place while God pours out the new wine. God selects the containers from which to pour out the new wine. Sometimes He will choose a brand-new wineskin that has never been used. But sometimes He asks an old wineskin to be renewed for the new wine. The process to make an old wineskin soft and supple is a time-consuming and rough process. The wineskin must have oil rubbed into the very essence of the wineskin, not just on the surface. This is done by pounding it with stones and stretching it on the ground. It is not instant, but is a painstaking process! Both the Psalmist (119:83) and Job (32:19) talked about feeling like an old wineskin filled with new wine when they were in the midst of the dealings of God. I know that feeling too!

The new wine is often full of violent reactions (fermentation). It is not stable and predictable. It is not known if the new wine will even fully mature to a good, mellow wine. But God does not want it lost just because the old wineskin will not contain it. New wine must be contained in a new or renewed wineskin. If we peek inside the wineskin filled with new wine, we might say that it is chaos and not God. Yet God created the world out of chaos.

God is asking some old wineskins (you and me) to go through the process of being renewed so that He can fill us with new wine.

God is asking some old wineskins (you and me) to go through the process of being renewed so that He can fill us with new wine. To those who don't understand, it will look painful (and it is) and chaotic (and it may be). But it also might be God. God is asking for friends of the bridegroom to be willing to look different from the world, and maybe even from old wineskins.

Living in Hope

While I was waiting in the doctor's office the other day, a magazine article on hopeful children caught my attention. In this uncertain world we live in, it is critical to be able to hope in God. We need to believe in someone greater than ourselves and to know that He is in control, when all else in the world has gone crazy. According to this article, hope is a learned behavior. Psychologists after years of zeroing in on people's weaknesses and problems are recognizing the importance of hope. Doesn't that sound like the church, too? The focus has been on "sin" and what I see wrong in you (criticalness) rather than what I see right in you (encouragement). God sees our hearts and focuses on what is right with each of us. He deals with sin in teachable moments to bring us to repentance. Don't get me wrong—God does have a high standard and does not condone sin. But He sees our willing hearts and applauds us in heaven. He wants us to learn to live in hope, no matter what circumstances come our way, because we intimately know the God of all the earth. The article stated that a child feels much more hopeful when he is working toward something bigger than himself. Our God is bigger than any problem, and our calling is to partner with His purposes! We need to trust Him! The article states that a hopeful parent is the best ways to instill hope in a child. Isn't it cool that regardless of how our natural parents raised us, we have a Father who is hopeful for us! *"For I know the thoughts that I think toward you, says the LORD, **thoughts of peace and not of evil, to give you a future and a hope**. Then you will call upon Me and go and pray to Me, and **I will listen to you**. And you will seek Me and find Me, when you search for Me with all your heart. **I will be found by you**, says the LORD, and **I will bring you back from your captivity**"* (Jeremiah 29:11–14, emphasis added).

Living in hope also affects how we walk with other people. God is calling us to join the great crowd of witnesses (Hebrews 12:1) to encourage each other, to keep pressing on even when the way is tough. God wants the members of His church, His Bride, to love one another. Let's increase in the gift of exhortation and let the enemy's gift of judgment decrease! Every person needs light and love spoken into him or her!

Friends of the Bridegroom

"Then there arose a dispute between some of John's

*disciples and the Jews about purification. And they came
to John and said to him, 'Rabbi, He who was with you
beyond the Jordan, to whom you have testified—behold,
He is baptizing, and all are coming to Him!' John
answered and said, 'A man can receive nothing unless it
has been given to him from heaven. You yourselves bear
me witness, that I said, "I am not the Christ," but, "I have
been sent before Him." **He who has the bride is the
bridegroom; but the friend of the bridegroom, who
stands and hears him, rejoices greatly because of the
bridegroom's voice.** Therefore this joy of mine is fulfilled.
He must increase, but I must decrease. He who comes
from above is above all; he who is of the earth is earthly
and speaks of the earth. **He who comes from heaven is
above all**'"* (John 3:25–31, emphasis added).

The three Synoptic Gospels (Matthew, Mark, and Luke) all give
the story of the new wineskins as a follow-on to the discussion on
the friends of the bridegroom. John the Baptist chose the above
story to explain his role as a friend of the bridegroom. Jesus is
joyfully anticipating the wedding with His bride (us). The friend of
the bridegroom rejoices with the bridegroom and the bride. The
focus during that season needs to be on the bridegroom and the
bride, not on their friends. It is their job to prepare (wash and dress)
the bride for the bridegroom and then escort her into the bridegroom's presence.

**God is raising up forerunners to prepare the
bride to fall passionately in love with her
bridegroom (Jesus).**

God is raising up forerunners to prepare the bride to fall passionately in love with her bridegroom (Jesus). Their focus is not on
themselves or their ministry, but on Jesus. God may require them to
look different from the Pharisees (the established church of the
times) or even from other forerunners. John was the greatest friend

of the bridegroom. He lived in the wilderness, wore a camel hair shirt, and ate locusts and wild honey. In response to the question, "What do you say about yourself?," he boldly proclaimed: *"I am 'The voice of one crying in the wilderness: "Make straight the way of the LORD," ' as the prophet Isaiah said."* (John 1:22–23). He was a voice in the wilderness calling to the people to repent of their sins and be baptized. Jesus' disciples looked and acted different from John the Baptist's disciples. Some of John's disciples became Jesus' disciples later.

We don't have a clue what the forerunners will look like. We only know that God will develop their voices or messages in the furnace of the wilderness, much as He has developed many great men and women of God. Moses, Joseph, Paul, Esther, and Deborah all went through times of preparation for their callings. Even Jesus, who was perfect man and perfect God, went through preparation in the wilderness. God deals uniquely with each individual because He knows us down to our essence—after all, He created us. He decides what needs to be purified and what needs to strengthened. His goal is to see His reflection in each of His people. Then we will be a bride without spot or wrinkle. You see, we are friends of the bridegroom and we are the bride. We must recognize the dual role.

First Commandment

God's desire from before the foundation of the earth was to have a people who would receive His love and then voluntarily and passionately love Him back. This is in the scriptures from Genesis to Revelation. He longs for us to *" 'love the LORD your God with all your heart, with all your soul, with all your strength, and with all your mind,' and 'your neighbor as yourself' "* (Luke 10:27). He wants us to make the first commandment first. Then we are to love our neighbors by preparing them to love the Lord with all their hearts, souls, minds, and strength. We do that by being real about God and ourselves. How do we become real? It is usually in the process of our old wineskins being renewed. We need to return to our first love—that time of emotional expectation for the beloved. It is when we are in this lover mode that we will be ready for the great harvest. We must be the lover who works as a result of love, not the servant who works and then loves only if he has the time. "Sacrifice is not the primary consideration for those who have been touched by the romance of the gospel, whose hearts are stirred by the beauty of God and who have a deep reality of love for God. Instead, such believers are caught up in the privilege of abandonment. Their primary reward is the power to love. Their reward is to feel and receive love, and then to reciprocate it by the power of God. They carry this reward within their hearts. Therefore, the Great Commission will move from a work paradigm of sacrificial labor to a love paradigm, an act of devotion of a lovesick bride. In this new paradigm, we carry the reward in our hearts because the first commandment is first."[2]

First things are first.

Forerunner Call

Merriam-Webster defines "forerunner" as "one that precedes and indicates the approach of another" as a "premonitory sign or symptom...".[3] The forerunner is one who prepares the world and the body of Christ for change as the time for Jesus' return approaches. Forerunners are paradigm changers. The world and the church are in transition. Change is evolving at faster and faster rates.

"The whole point of leadership and ministry is to produce a body of people capable of doing the work."[4] This represents leadership in the church and in the marketplace. God is calling His people to live by faith. We see in part; therefore, we must be totally dependent on God to show us how to bring the vision to fruition. In the past, we as God's people saw part of the vision and then ran to fulfill it the best way we could. Often, we not only thought we knew how to perform it best, but that God couldn't get it done if we didn't do it! This is presumption! God doesn't need us to fulfill His vision! He gives us the privilege to partner with Him to bring forth what He envisions. "The key to our ability to change is a changeless sense of who we are in Christ, what we value in spiritual terms, and what we are about in the purposes of God. It is always about our identity, the nature of God, and the vision for the kingdom."[5] God is in the business of transforming us; this is the purpose for the wilderness. It is to change our priorities, wants, and desires into His priorities, wants, and desires.

"The forerunner ministries of the kingdom of God are now being released throughout the earth. The Lord has hidden away and prepared those who will preach the gospel of the kingdom with power. Their time has now come. They will be released in waves, with each wave being more powerful than the preceding one. The power of their words will bring righteousness, peace, and joy right in the midst of the greatest unrighteousness, conflict, and depression the world has ever known.... The weapon of this army is the truth that is spoken in love, bringing healing."[6]

Walking in His Ways

Psalm 103:7 states, *"He made known His ways to Moses, His acts to the children of Israel."* God spoke to Moses face to face, which speaks of intimacy. For years, I have prayed with Moses, *"Now therefore, **I pray, if I have found grace in Your sight, show me now Your way, that I may know You and that I may find grace in Your sight.** And consider that this nation is Your people"* (Exodus 33:13, emphasis added). My heart cry is to know Him so well that I recognize when He is at work in my life or the world. The rest of Israel only knew of His acts because they did not go daily into the tent of meeting. I don't want to be a "watcher" of God; I want to be immersed in His presence.

"Superficiality is the curse of our age. The doctrine of instant satisfaction is a primary spiritual problem. The desperate need today is not for a greater number of intelligent people, or gifted people, but for deep people."[7] The call of God is for us to be authentic or real, and to go deeply into Him by learning His ways. The Lord spoke, "Know me and walk in My ways. Be willing to be a path finder and one who marks the path for others to follow. It is as you walk and run in the untrodden places that you will find yourself and a deeper place in me. I am the path (way) and you will experience joy as you find me in the hidden and unexpected places. I ask you to have an expectancy as you travel the new."

The Bible doesn't discuss Enoch much. But it does say Enoch walked with God for three hundred years! For most of us, walking with God on the earth for about 70 years is only an appetizer for what we will experience with God in heaven. Apparently Enoch's walk with God was so close that he didn't die. He just went to heaven. Hmmm.... *"Enoch lived sixty-five years, and begot Methuselah.*

After he begot Methuselah, **Enoch walked with God three hundred years,** *and had sons and daughters. So all the days of Enoch were three hundred and sixty-five years. And* **Enoch walked with God; and he was not, for God took him** *"* (Genesis 5:21–24, emphasis added). What did he know that we don't? I believe he was so addicted to the presence of God that He couldn't stand to be separated from Him. God gave him his heart's desire. Adam and Eve had that same sort of fellowship in the Garden of Eden before they fell and were expelled. Jesus has reversed the curse so that we can be restored to close fellowship today. How hungry are you for this type of fellowship with God?

What we believe matters. But how we choose to live out that belief also matters. Our walk with God is about the choices we make.

What we believe matters. But how we choose to live out that belief also matters. Our walk with God is about the choices we make. We can choose selfishness and self-righteousness, or we can choose to die to self so that God can increase in our lives. *"But if we walk in the light as He is in the light, we have fellowship with one another, and the blood of Jesus Christ His Son cleanses us from all sin"* (1 John 1:7). The word "walk" in Hebrew means a well-worn path, or our daily habits. Does how we live bring glory to ourselves, to the enemy of our soul, or to God? If someone were a fly on the wall, would he say that our lives bring glory to God as we shop in a crowded store, when we are stressed at work, or when we are sitting at home with "no one" watching? Would he know that we experience God's deep love for us and that we love God? This is where the rubber meets the road. What do our lifestyles say about God and who we are? Not a single person, myself included, has arrived or makes all the right choices! I am grateful that God looks at our hearts to see what our desires are and not just our performance. He has far more grace and mercy than I do! This is why we must have hearts that lean upon Him and depend on Him for direction. We need to know His voice and His ways! The first step on that path is to know how much the God of all the universe loves me and you, whether or not you know Him intimately.

God's Desire

What has God desired since before He created time and the foundation of the earth? Yahweh has been longing for a people who will passionately respond to His love. They will willingly call Him their God and let Him call them His people. This is the call to every individual person on earth as well as to corporate bodies of people, be they congregations, nations, people groups, or corporate businesses. *"I will give them a heart to know me, that I am the LORD. They will be my people, and I will be their God, for they will return to me with all their heart"* (Jeremiah 24:7). (Also Genesis 17:8, 31:1, 31:33, 32:38; Ezekiel 11:20, 14:11, 37:23, 37:27; Zechariah 8:8; 2 Corinthians 6:16; and Hebrews 8:10).

Although I am not married, I know one of the deepest longings in my heart is to love someone with my whole heart and to be loved passionately by him. Why does this longing exist in every person on earth? It is because God put this into our very DNA, because we are created in His image. (Genesis 1:27: *"So God created man in his own image, in the image of God he created him; male and female he created them."*) I have waited a long time for God to bring my husband into my life. Part of that time God was preparing me to be a bride for God first and my natural husband second. In addition, He wanted me to experience a small piece of God's longing for a bride that is "heart of his heart." I have come to recognize what I desire in a husband (and I know it is a tall order). Here it is:

1. A man who is passionate about God and people, and is unafraid to express that passion.

2. A man who is on the same page spiritually as I am. We are able to share the deepest things in our hearts, those precious treasures that God shares with us in our times of intimacy with Him.

3. A man of upright character who I can trust fully, and who trusts me fully.

4. A man who is authentic. He can fully be himself with me, and I can fully be myself with him.

5. A man who laughs and knows how to rejoice and have fun with me.

As I prayed about this person, I recognized that what I desired was a man who had the character and nature of God burned into his very fiber. Then God began to speak that this is what He desires in His Bride—individuals and corporate entities who clearly reflect who He is. They trust Him so much that they will follow Him to the ends of the earth AND to the cross so He can remove the filth from their lives. They will be quick to be obedient to what He says. They are free to be unashamed before Him because they know that they have been redeemed and His glory shines from them.

God began to speak that this is what He desires in His Bride—individuals and corporate entities who clearly reflect who He is.

In the Beginning

In the beginning of the Bible, God states that He wanted a perfect companion for Adam: *"The Lord God said, 'It is not good for the man to be alone. I will make a helper suitable for him.' ... But for Adam no suitable helper was found. So the Lord God caused the man to fall into a deep sleep; and while he was sleeping, he took one of the man's ribs and closed up the place with flesh. Then the*

Lord God made a woman from the rib he had taken out of the man, and he brought her to the man. The man said, 'This is now bone of my bones and flesh of my flesh; she shall be called "woman," for she was taken out of man.' For this reason a man will leave his father and mother and be united to his wife, and they will become one flesh. The man and his wife were both naked, and they felt no shame" (Genesis 2:18–25).

From the beginning of time, God has been concerned that each person has a perfect mate. Adam had one in the natural realm (Eve) and one in the spiritual realm (God Himself). I often wonder about Adam—*if* he had fully comprehended his love relationship with God, would mankind's fall have happened? Or if Adam and Eve had been truly focused on pleasing God first and each other second, would the temptations of the serpent have had no effect? This is just one of those things I wonder about. Of course, I recognize the love relationship I have with God, but I *still* do things I know I shouldn't. But then I don't live in a perfect world. Hmmm... I wonder..., anyway.

Marriage as a Biblical Theme

The Song of Solomon, part of the wisdom literature of the Bible, speaks intimately of the love relationship between a man and a woman, but also between God and His bride. In 7:10, the Shulamite woman (representing us) exults, *"I belong to my lover, and his desire is for me."* God longs to hear us say that of our relationship with Him.

Paul of Tarsus gives this same analogy in the New Testament. Paul studied under Gamaliel (one of the most renowned Rabbis (teachers) of that time period) so he knew the word of God. In Ephesians 5:25–33, Paul commands husbands to love their wives the same way that *Yeshua* loves the church. God is jealous over the church to become her very best: *"Husbands, love your wives, just as **Christ loved the church** and gave himself up for her to make her holy, cleansing her by the washing with water through the word, and to **present her to himself as a radiant church, without stain or wrinkle or any other blemish, but holy and blameless**. In this same way, husbands ought to love their wives as their own bodies. He who loves his wife loves himself. After all, no one ever hated his own body, but he feeds and cares for it, **just as Christ does the*** *church—for we are members of his body. 'For this reason a man will leave his father and mother and be united to his wife, and **the two will become one flesh.' This is a profound mystery—but I am talking about Christ and the church**. However, each one of you also must love his wife as he loves himself, and the wife must respect her husband"* (emphasis added).

Even the end of the last book of the Bible, Revelation, speaks of this theme. John the Apostle was in a trance and the Spirit took him to see past, present, and future events. This is the denouement or culmination of God's purposes for the people of the earth:

> *I saw the Holy City, the New Jerusalem, **coming down out of heaven from God, prepared as a bride beautifully dressed for her husband**. And I heard a loud voice from the throne saying, "Now the **dwelling of God is with men**, and he will live with them. **They will be his people, and God himself will be with them and be their God**. He will wipe every tear from their eyes. There will be no more death or mourning or crying or pain, for **the old order of things has passed away**." He who was seated on the throne said, "I am making everything new!" Then he said, "Write this down, for these words are trustworthy and true." He said to me: "It is done. I am the Alpha and the Omega, the Beginning and the End. To him who is thirsty I will give to drink without cost from the spring of the water of life. **He who overcomes will inherit all this, and I will be his God and he will be my son**. But the cowardly, the unbelieving, the vile, the murderers, the sexually immoral, those who practice magic arts, the idolaters and all liars—their place will be in the fiery lake of burning sulfur. This is the second death." One of the seven angels who had the seven bowls full of the seven last plagues came and said to me, "**Come, I will show you the bride, the wife of the Lamb.**" And he carried me away in the Spirit to a mountain great and high, and showed me the Holy City, Jerusalem, coming down out of heaven from God. **It shone with the glory of God**, and its brilliance was like that of a very precious jewel, like a jasper, clear*

*as crystal. It had a great, high wall with twelve gates, and with twelve angels at the gates. On the gates were written the names of the **twelve tribes of Israel**. There were three gates on the east, three on the north, three on the south and three on the west. The wall of the city had twelve foundations, and on them were the names of the **twelve apostles of the Lamb**.* (Revelation 21:2–14, emphasis added)

The bride of *Yeshua* (Jesus) **is** the New Jerusalem, which is a community that reflects the glory of God. She is composed of Jews and Gentiles. She is filled with overcomers who have accepted *Yeshua* as God and have become His sons and daughters, regardless of their nationalities, creeds, or races.

This theme of God's love for a people who will voluntarily respond in love to Him is found from Genesis to Revelation.

This theme of God's love for a people who will voluntarily respond in love to Him is found from Genesis to Revelation. The Bible is truly a love story. But we won't see the finale until we are all in heaven.

The Bride

God had a dream for Himself—a loving bride. Since Adam was created in God's image, God knew Adam needed a wife—a counterpart.

Gene Edwards in *The Divine Romance* and Kay Arthur in *Beloved Israel* take this on-again, off-again love affair between God and His people described throughout scripture and use their divinely given imagination to describe this romance.

I am going to quote five sections from the *Divine Romance* because they capture the essence of what God wants to communicate about His desire for a people who would return His love. Read and listen to these segments with your heart, not just your mind. Some parts may challenge what you have previously been taught!

God's Dream

This first section[8] describes the dream of God's heart:

> In this non-time of so long ago, there was but one life form... the highest life.
>
> *He was also love.*
>
> Passionate, emotional, expressive ... love.
>
> In this God, dwelling so alone, there was a paradox: though he was alone, he was also love. Yet there was no *counterpart* for him to love. A love so vast, so powerful, yet, there was no "other than."
>
> Then life pulsated, light blazed in newfound glory as revelation ascended in him, as he cried from within the council of the Godhead.
>
> *There can be two!*
>
> "I ... the living God ... shall have a *counterpart!*"
>
> Exulting in the revelation, he consecrated his whole being to this one task: to have ... *a bride.* For one brief moment the infinite solitude retreated.
>
> But just before he launched his grand design, a very mysterious thing took place *in* God. Deep within the center of his being there occurred an event that no other eye was to see, no other mind to conceive.
>
> A thousand million portions of God burst upward in light. Each of these portions of God ignited in flaming brilliance ... as if to proclaim that each had been chosen— even *marked off*—for some special, distant destiny. Having marked off these future destinies, the living God gave himself to making real his highest dream. Unending self-containment would end.

Love Given AND Received

In describing the relationship between Adam and Eve, God also gives the hint of his heartbeat:[9]

> "Your substance has been divided, man. Yet it remains the same. She is of you, out of you, from you, and one with you ... yet now separate.

"You are, and ever shall be, my image. Therefore she must return to you, this substance of your substance. She must become, once more, *one* with *you*."

"I do not fully understand all that you have said," replied the man slowly.

"It is not necessary that you understand. But it is important that you pour out your love on her. For now at last, your love has somewhere to go."

Betraying some hidden doubt, man responded, "I have never expressed this love that beats within me. Will I..."

"I have fashioned from your being a *she*. And, yes, you will know how to express that love that is now still captured within you."

"And... and then?"

"Counterpart will, of course, return that love to you."

The man stopped. "You mean," he responded, stunned at the idea now coursing through him, "you mean that love shall not only be given, but shall also be *received*? Love will be returned?"

The Lord's own being trembled at the word. "Yes. Given ... *and* received," he replied.... "There resides in the council of my being an exchange of fellowship ... and of love about which you know nothing. *Within* my being courses a love of Fatherhood and Sonhood ... of which you are but a reflection. The depth and breadth of *this* love is beyond all mortal conception. But the love of a counterpart ... This is a matter of discovery you will know and I shall never ... It is a matter you will know *before* I know!"

Love God!

Moses describes the Lord seeing Israel as a young woman that He is wooing and teaching.[10] God instructed Moses to teach Israel how to respond in love to Him:

"It is to *you* that the Lord has turned his great love. But be not proud. For it is not that you are a fair and noble people that he loves you. No! For you are the sons and daughters of slaves, a people despised. Nor is it because

21

you are a great and large nation that he loves you. No! For you are the smallest of nations.

"Then why does he love you?

"He loves you ... because he loves you.

"Today we journey once again toward that land that the Lord gave to our father, Abraham. When you have entered that land, you will grow strong and prosper. In that day, do not forget your God. Turn not to the ways of the nations surrounding you. Fill that land with iniquity as the other nations fill theirs, and you will surely learn the Lord's displeasure. Even his wrath....

"I have stood before him, face to face. I have seen his holiness ... yet lived! I have watched his power ... unlimited. I have drowned in his glory ... indescribable. What does such a God require of us? But *one* thing. Above all else, one thing." Moses then cried out,

Love him
With all your might,
Love him
With all your mind,
Love him
With all your soul,
Love him
With all your being.
Love him!

Miracle of Love's Scar

Jesus' resurrection[11] reveals how our relationship with Him was changed in a moment. So that which was outside of time was finally able to come forth in time:

Now came a thunderous shout ... from within the tomb!
"I am alive!"

Instantly, without thought or instinct, this man rising out of the sleep of death—like the first man Adam had done before him—grabbed his side.

"A scar! A scar on my side!

"Something is *missing* from *me*! Something ... someone ... that has been inside me for all eternity is now missing!"

He rose up *through* the grave cloth, sprang to his feet, and flung off the headpiece.

"Divisible! I have become divisible.

"She who was hidden in me for all eternity ... she has come forth from my side.

"Bone of my bone ... flesh of ...

"Nay!" He roared. "Spirit of my Spirit, life of my Life ... essence of my Essence," he exclaimed, raising both arms high above his head in exultation.

It is true, you see, that if one should thrust his hand into the earth, he will surely bring forth earth. And if one should thrust his hand into the side of man, he will surely bring forth humanity. And, perchance, should one thrust his hand into the side of God, he will surely bring forth divinity!

Something of God had come forth from God, just as surely as something of Adam had come forth from Adam. As Eve was the substance of Adam, so was someone, somewhere substance of *him*.

Ironic, is it not, that the singular, most perfect creature in all the universe—standing there in a translated body radiating all the light of the glory of God—had upon his side ... *a scar*! The evidence of the price he had paid for a counterpart.

Love's Ultimate Mystery

Finally we have a description of the unveiling of the bride in heaven.[12] I love a good mystery book because "when all is revealed," I want to know if I figured it out. That sense of anticipation of the unveiling is what God has placed within each of us.

That sense of anticipation of the unveiling is what God has placed within each of us.

When the Lord created Eve, he was "seeing" *someone* else. He had fashioned Eve in the image of an exotically beautiful woman who belonged to some other dimension.

That woman now stood before them. There was no question, Eve was but the foreshadowing of *this one*. Before them stood a woman of incomparable glory and beauty, made up of the unnumbered portions of God's own being—portions of God chosen, before the foundations of the ages, to be the composites of her being.

Here, at last, was the Mystery *who* had been hidden in God!

Angels hardly dared to look upon such terrible beauty, yet they dared not do otherwise.

Here was a woman, robed in the very brightness and glory of God, within a beauty defying their comprehension. She was like *him*, yet female! A loveliness so tender, a countenance so full of love, a being so pure that angelic eyes shone with awe and terror seeking to take it in. She had been formed out of God. She did not belong to creation, for he is uncreated. And, as Eve was bone of Adam's bone, this woman was spirit of the Lord's Spirit. The uncreated God had revealed to them his counterpart. A woman fashioned out of the water and spirit of an uncreated God, being of his being.

Her hair was black as ravens, her youth had once inspired a creating God to fashion springtime. Her features encompassed all the beauty of every race and tribe and kindred of womanhood from all the ends of creation, for each of them had been but a portion, a picture of her.

My Beginning

In July 1971, my life started again. I had been severely depressed and suicidal. I felt that life had no meaning and I was not loved for myself. As a way of escaping, I read voraciously. One day I "happened" to pick up *The Cross and the Switchblade*. It was the story of David Wilkerson's conversion from being an average pastor to a radical, on-fire Christian. The part that hit my heart was the confrontation between David and Nicky Cruz. Nicky carried a switchblade and screamed at David, "I'll kill you." And David calmly responded, "You could do that. You could cut me in a thousand pieces and lay them out in the street and every piece would love you."[13] I wanted a love that real. I wanted to know God loved me like that, so I could love others like that. I wanted a love that would transform me. After finishing the book, I set up a small table with a little plastic statue of Jesus. I whispered, "God, if you are real, I ask you to come into my heart." He answered and came into my heart. It took awhile for my heart to melt so that I could feel God's love, but it was real.

How About You?

Do you know this God who loves you? Is it time for you to respond to Him in a new way? Do you want to be one who He calls "My child"? Do you want to be sought by God as a bridegroom pursues his bride?

If you answered affirmatively to the above questions, or even want to know more, I invite you to read and then pray the prayer below:

> Jesus, I want to know You and let You know me down in the depths of who I am. I want to be called one of Your people. I am tired of looking for love in all the wrong places. I want my heart to be settled. I choose to seek after You, God. I invite You to come and live in my life today and forever more. I choose You as my one and only God. Change my heart so I can fully embrace You and Your people. I want to be changed by You. Teach me how to walk in Your ways daily that I might please You all the days of my life. I choose life, blessing, and joy! Thank You, God, for what You have done this day.

What About the Bride?

If God has desired a bride for His Son since before time, what is she to be like? What sort of character is she to have to be worthy of the Son of God?

The prophets were God's voice to the people of Israel. Often He called them to be visual pictures of what God was speaking to His people at a particular point in time. The prophet Hosea, whose name means "salvation" or "deliverance," was chosen by God to be a living illustration of how God felt He was being treated by Israel. Hosea 1:2: *"When the Lord began to speak through Hosea, the Lord said to him, 'Go, take to yourself an adulterous wife and children of unfaithfulness, because the land is guilty of the vilest adultery in departing from the Lord.'"* God asked Hosea to represent Himself and Hosea's wife to represent the House of Israel. Hosea married a prostitute to illustrate God's commitment to Israel despite her unfaithfulness to Yahweh. Now that is commitment to God and marriage!

Merriam-Webster defines "adultery" as: "voluntary sexual intercourse between a married man and someone other than his wife or between a married woman and someone other than her husband."[14] God claims Israel had committed spiritual adultery. Spiritual adultery is breaking our "marriage" covenant with God by trusting in and worshipping other gods. It is done by no longer walking in God's ways. Spiritual adultery can be overt, by actively worshipping other gods, or it can be subtle, by paying more attention or giving our hearts to activities such as sports, work, or other people. God wants us to give Him our hearts first and foremost. In a human marriage, when one party is unfaithful (commits adultery), it is legal grounds for a divorce. The injured party is no longer required to provide housing, food, or a relationship. So when God's people commit spiritual adultery, God no longer **promises** to provide for our basic needs.

Wow! That's a heavy definition—loving anyone or anything more than God!

Faithfulness

Hosea's wife was named Gomer. She had three children. Each had a prophetic name that described God's progressive unhappiness with Israel:

1. **Jezreel** means "God scatters" or "God sows." God is prophetically declaring that he will scatter and sow the Northern Kingdom of Israel into the nations as a result of their spiritual adultery.

2. **Lo-Ruhamah** means "No mercy." It indicates that God is removing his compassion and mercy from the House of Israel, the Northern Kingdom. Judgment is coming. At this time, God in His mercy was not planning on judging the House of Judah, the Southern Kingdom. The Northern Kingdom, the remaining eleven tribes, were to be judged.

3. **Lo-Ammi** means "Not my people." "For you are not My people and I will not be your God." God was declaring a divorce. The Northern Kingdom of Israel would no longer be God's special people because of their lifestyle choices.

Hosea was heartbroken over Gomer's inability to remain faithful to him, just as God grieved over the unfaithfulness of Israel to Him. Since God is also a God of justice, He was required to expose her actions to give Israel the opportunity to change and return to Him. But most of all, He is saying Israel, "My beloved, I once called you **My people**, but now I am calling you **Not my people** in the hope that you will return to Me as your faithful husband."

Perhaps this is God's version of tough love. It is very strong language. The bottom line is that God will not only stop blessing her, but He will block her path with thorn bushes to wall her in. He rebukes her for not understanding that the very things she offered to the other gods (grain, new wine, oil, silver, and gold) were all gifts from God Himself.

> *Rebuke your mother, rebuke her, for* **she is not my wife, and I am not her husband.** *Let her remove the adulterous look from her face and the unfaithfulness from between her breasts. Otherwise I will strip her naked and make her as bare as on the day she was born; I will make her like a desert, turn her into a parched land, and slay her with thirst. I will not show my love to her children, because they are the children of adultery.* **Their mother has been unfaithful** *and has conceived them in disgrace. She said, "I will go after my lovers, who give me my food and my water, my wool and my linen, my oil and my drink." Therefore I will block her path with thorn bushes;* **I will wall her in** *so that she cannot find her way. She will chase after her lovers but not catch them; she will look for them but not find them. Then she will say, "I will go back to my husband as at first, for then I was better off than now."* **She has not acknowledged that I was the one who gave her the grain, the new wine and oil, who lavished on her the silver and gold**—*which they used for Baal.* (Hosea 2:2–8, emphasis added)

God the Father's desire is for a faithful bride for His son.

Hope for Renewed Passion

God loves Israel so much that He will woo her, in the hope that she will return to Him desiring intimacy, not just the material comforts she lusts after. He is willing to take her into the wilderness so that she will recognize her isolation and long to be with God in new ways. God wants her to obey Him **not** out of duty as a slave to a master, but as a beloved who wants to please her lover. God is calling her to be "head over heels" in love, as is evident during the betrothal. **Then** God will covenant with her once more. His desire is not for judgment. For if she will return to Him and call Him her God, He will give her all she needs. He will have mercy on her, and call her "My people" once more! But that blessing is conditional upon her positive response to Him. In many cultures, the betrothal period was the key to the rest of a bride's life.

God loves Israel so much that He will woo her, in the hope that she will return to Him desiring intimacy.

---

*"Therefore **I am now going to allure her**; I will lead her into the desert and speak tenderly to her. There I will give her back her vineyards, and will make the Valley of Achor a door of hope. There she will sing as in the days of her youth, as in the day she came up out of Egypt. **In that day," declares the Lord, "you will call me 'my husband'; you will no longer call me 'my master.'** I will remove the names of the Baals from her lips; no longer will their names be invoked. In that day I will make a covenant for them with the beasts of the field and the birds of the air and the creatures that move along the ground. Bow and sword and battle I will abolish from the land, so that all may lie down in safety. **I will betroth you to me forever; I will betroth** you in righteousness and justice, in love and compassion. **I will betroth** you in faithfulness, and you will acknowledge the Lord. In that day I will respond," declares the Lord—"I will respond to the skies, and they will respond to the earth; and the earth will respond to the grain, the new wine and oil, and they will respond to Jezreel. I will plant her for myself in the land; **I will show my love to the one I called 'Not my loved one.' I will say to those called 'Not my people,' 'You are my people'; and they will say, 'You are my God'"* (Hosea 2:14–23, emphasis added).

The betrothal is a time for the man and woman to get to know each other intimately, other than physically. Merriam-Webster's defines "intimate" as: "**1 a : INTRINSIC, ESSENTIAL b :** belonging to or characterizing one's deepest nature **2 :** marked by very close association, contact, or familiarity <*intimate* knowledge of the law> **3 a :** marked by a warm friendship developing through long association **b :** suggesting informal warmth or privacy <*intimate* clubs> **4 :** of a very personal or private nature."[15] God is looking for a long-term relationship where we know the essentials, the deepest nature of who He is. He wants us to desire to know what He feels and says. But He also wants us to open up with Him and be honest about who we are (the good, the bad, and the ugly). He already knows us, so why pretend? No matter what we do, God is longing for us to call Him "My God" and "My husband" so that He can call us "His People."

Knowing God

Chapters 3–13 of Hosea outline God's charges against Israel, her impending judgment, and her call to repentance through the prophet Hosea.

Hosea 4:6 and 14:9 are keys to understanding why God is accusing Israel of spiritual adultery: *"My people are destroyed from **lack of knowledge**. Because you have **rejected knowledge**, I also reject you as my priests; because you have **ignored the law of your God**, I also will ignore your children"* (4:6, emphasis added). *"Who is **wise**? He will realize these things. Who is **discerning**? He will **understand** them. The ways of the Lord are right; the righteous walk in them, but the rebellious stumble in them"* (14:9, emphasis added).

In the above two passages, God is saying because the Israelite people have rejected a personal **knowledge** of the living God and His *Torah*, God will reject them. *Torah* is often translated as "law" but it actually means God's teaching and instruction. The people **know** the way to walk before God as outlined in the *Torah*, but they have chosen another way. The wise, the discerning, and understanding will *know* that God's ways are right and will follow them.

Yada is used for the most intimate acquaintance. God knows Moses face to face

---

The Hebrew word for knowledge is *da'at* from the root *yada,* "to know." *Yada* occurs 944 times and is used to express many of shades of knowledge gained by the senses. The closest synonyms are "to discern" and "to recognize." "Yada is used to describe God's knowledge of man (Genesis 18:19; Deuteronomy 34:10) and of his ways (Isaiah 48:8, Psalms 1:6 and 37:18) which begins even before birth (Jeremiah 1:5). **Yada is used for the most intimate acquaintance.** God knows Moses face to face (Exodus 33:17, Deuteronomy 34:10). He knows the Psalmist's sitting and rising (Psalms 139:2). Yada is also used for sexual intercourse in the well-known euphemism 'Adam knew Eve his wife' and its parallels (Genesis 4:1, 19:8, Numbers 31:17,35, Judges 11:39, 21:11, 1 Kings 1:4, 1 Samuel 1:19)."[16] *Yada* describes knowledge or a lack of knowledge of the divine, either Jehovah or other gods.

Da'at is used ninety-three times in the Old Testament. ***Da'at* is a general term for knowledge, particularly that which is of a personal and experiential nature** (Proverbs 24:5). It often refers to technical knowledge, such as the ability to build the Tabernacle or Temple. This word is also used for the moral cognition, which came from the tree of the knowledge of good and evil. It is also used numerous times in the prophetic concept "knowledge of God," which is particularly prominent in the book of Hosea. Knowledge of God came to certain individuals in the Bible when God revealed Himself personally, such as Abraham and Moses. This revelation or teaching was then taught to other individuals. Thus the revelation of God's ways was passed down from generation to generation. The prophetic view of the Messianic age is of a time when the knowledge of God covers the earth as the waters cover the sea.[17]

Hosea 6:1–3 gives the promise that God will heal the people, if they acknowledge Him. This is the word *yada. "Come, let us return to the Lord. He has torn us to pieces but he will heal us; he has injured us but he will bind up our wounds. After two days he will revive us; on the third day **he will restore us, that we may live in*** *his presence. Let us **acknowledge** the Lord; let us press on to **acknowledge** him. As surely as the sun rises, he will appear; he will come to us like the winter rains, like the spring rains that water the earth"* (emphasis added). The reason God wants to heal us is so we can live in His presence continually.

Righteousness

In Hosea 10:12, God charges us to sow righteous deeds so that He can shower righteousness on His people. Basically, it is time for a change in lifestyle! *"Sow for yourselves righteousness, reap the fruit of unfailing love, and break up your unplowed ground; for it is time to seek the Lord, until he comes and showers righteousness on you."*

Tsadeq is the Hebrew word for righteousness and justice. The root connotes conformity to an ethical or moral standard, and that standard is the nature and will of God.[18] God wants a people who will be walking examples of who He is. He wants a people who live according to His righteousness, rather than merely saying that they believe in His righteousness. Actions speak louder than words. Righteousness is living in accordance with who God is.

Complete Trust

God is calling for a complete trust in Him. When we know God and wait for Him, we are not dependent on dishonest or unrighteous ways. We walk in the simplicity of integrity and humility. *"But you must return to your God; maintain love and justice, and wait for your God always. The merchant uses dishonest scales; he loves to defraud. Ephraim boasts, 'I am very rich; I have become wealthy. With all my wealth they will not find in me any iniquity or sin'"* (Hosea 12:6–8).

God is not against wealth. But He is against those who have obtained wealth through unrighteous or ungodly means or love money too much. *"For the love of money is a root of all kinds of evil, for which some have strayed from the faith in their greediness, and pierced themselves through with many sorrows"* (1 Timothy 6:10).

Holiness

Holiness in the strictest sense means to be set apart by a holy God. Throughout scripture, God is called "Holy, Holy, Holy." God displayed His presence in the Old and New Testaments in very dramatic ways that often meant trouble to those who had not prepared themselves to meet a holy God! Often angels appeared saying, "Do not fear!" because the natural reaction was fear and trembling. But the two characteristics that most describe a holy God are justice and mercy. In our small brains we think these are opposites. However, they are two sides of His holiness.

"Divine holiness allows God the freedom to act in unexpected ways. Thus in Hosea 11:9, after an agonizing reflection on Israel's unfaithfulness, God determines not to execute justice on Israel, as one might expect, but rather mercy. *'I will not execute the fierceness of My anger; I will not again destroy Ephraim. For I am God, and not man, the Holy One in your midst; And I will not come with terror.'* Here the holiness of God becomes the basis for God's freedom to act in gracious ways when one might expect only judgment."[19]

God's call to Israel in the midst of judgment is to receive His beauty so they might be revived.

However, God still wants us to *"Be holy, for I am holy"* (1 Peter 1:16). Just like the description of Israel in Hosea, I don't feel very holy at times. In fact, like David, it often seems that *"my sin is always before me"* (Psalm 51:3).

God sets the standard, but He is the Papa in heaven who is pleased with each small child's step of progress on the road of holiness. He examines our hearts, not just our actions.

God's Beauty

God's call to Israel in the midst of judgment is to receive His beauty so they might be revived. Many of the descriptors God gives for Himself are reflected in what they shall be like. The end of the book is a beautiful promise of restoration and being conformed to His image:

> *O Israel, return to the LORD your God, For **you have stumbled because of your iniquity**; Take words with you,*

*And return to the LORD. Say to Him, "Take away all iniquity; **Receive us graciously**, For we will offer the sacrifices of our lips. Assyria shall not save us, We will not ride on horses, **Nor will we say anymore to the work of our hands, 'You are our gods.' For in You the father-less finds mercy."** "I will heal their backsliding, **I will love them freely**, For My anger has turned away from him. **I will be like the dew to Israel; He shall grow like the lily**, And lengthen his roots like Lebanon. His branches shall spread; **His beauty shall be like an olive tree**, And **his fragrance like Lebanon. Those who dwell under his shadow shall return; They shall be revived like grain**, and grow like a vine. **Their scent** shall be like the wine of Lebanon. Ephraim shall say, 'What have I to do anymore with idols?' I have heard and observed him. I am like a green cypress tree; your fruit is found in Me." Who is wise? Let him understand these things. Who is prudent? Let him know them. **For the ways of the LORD are right; The righteous walk in them**, But transgressors stumble in them.* (Hosea 14:1–9, emphasis added)

Israel, the bride, is so lovesick for God that she throws away the idolatry in her life and no longer trusts in her own strength (horses). She is a passionate bride in love with her bridegroom. This lovesickness causes her to live a very different life. Many of the themes in this section point to the beauty themes in the Song of Solomon. It is a return to focusing on the bridegroom while giving up fascination with things of the world.

Passing Over to
a New Way of Life

On the eve of the new millennium, God asked me, "Why is this night different from all others?" This is one of the questions the youngest child asks during the Passover Seder. So a friend and I started meditating on Passover.

Passover

Passover is the story of the deliverance of the nation of Israel from the slavery of Pharaoh. "Passover" in Hebrew is from the root *pesach,* to pass over. *Pesach* means "not to 'pass over' per se, but rather 'to defend, protect.' The Lord will protectively cover the houses of the Israelites and will not suffer the destroyer to enter."[20]

"Passover was originally a feast for those about to be delivered by their direct obedience to the covenant God; it served as the final dynamic proof of God's presence and protective care. Its continued celebration by all the congregation of Israel would serve as a memorial for those who had been delivered and their offspring. It is celebrated the ninth day of the fourth month, Nisan. It marks the new year because it was the beginning of a new life as a people. It is characterized by selecting a perfect lamb, which is sacrificed four days later and eaten as part of a major commemorative meal. A feast of hope and new life, the Passover represents deliverance and new beginnings; in many of its elements, it is a type of Christ, our Redeemer, the Lamb of God."[21]

Redemption and Relationship

God told Moses to speak different things to the Israelites and to Pharaoh. To the Israelites, he spoke about relationship and redemption. It was one of the many times God called to them to be His people and for them to choose Him as their God. However, the people of Israel were too downtrodden from a lifetime of slavery to hear the invitation. Israel's test was, "Do you believe I can do this?"

> *"Therefore, say to the Israelites: 'I am the Lord, and I will bring you out from under the yoke of the Egyptians.* **I will free you from being slaves to them, and I will redeem you with an outstretched arm and with mighty acts of judgment. I will take you as my own people, and I will be your God. Then you will know that I am the Lord your God**, *who brought you out from under the yoke of the Egyptians. And I will bring you to the land I swore with uplifted hand to give to Abraham, to Isaac and to Jacob. I will give it to you as a possession. I am the Lord.'"* Moses reported this to the Israelites, but **they did not listen to him because of their discouragement and cruel bondage.** (Exodus 6:6–9, emphasis added)

On the other hand, the Lord showed His strong right hand to Pharaoh in miracles and two plagues, before scripture records any dialogue between Moses and Pharaoh. Before the second, fourth, fifth, and seventh plagues, God instructs Moses to speak to Pharaoh, *"This is what the Lord says:* **Let my people go, so that they may worship me.** *If you refuse to let them go I will plague your whole country with...."* (Exodus 8:1–2, 8:20–21, 9:1–2, 9:13–14, and 10:4–5). It was the fourth plague (flies) when God began to distinguish between His people and the Egyptians. *"I will make a distinction between my people and your people. This miraculous sign will occur tomorrow"* (Exodus 8:23). God performed these miracles so they would believe in Him and break free from the Egyptian anti-God culture. The book of Revelation also depicts plagues. The Exodus plagues give us a picture of their role in Moses' time and as a study for what will happen in the last days.

I believe God did not start distinguishing the Israelites as "His people" until they started believing in their hearts that He was their God. Even Pharaoh's magicians recognized the finger of God before the Israelites (8:19). In an effort to compromise, Pharaoh tempts Moses three times to accept lesser conditions than what God spoke (8:25, 28; 10:10–11; 10:24). Moses stood firm for all that God spoke. God hardened the heart of Pharaoh, because He had another purpose. He wanted Pharaoh, his officials, and the people of Egypt *"to fear the Lord God"* (9:30) and to be humbled (10:3), just as God wanted His people to do the same. The Israelites were being released from slavery not just for the sake of freedom, but so they could worship the Lord God Almighty. They needed to see God move deliberately on their behalf, so their hearts could be softened to believe Him.

"To fear God is to obey Him, even when it does not seem to be to our advantage. When we fear Him, He calls us *friend*, and reveals the *why*, or the intentions of His heart. We come to know Him not by His acts but by His ways."[22] Moses knew God's ways, and saw God face to face. Israel knew His acts. Pharaoh wasn't even able to acknowledge His acts. *"He made known His ways to Moses, His acts to the children of Israel"* (Psalm 103:7). Acts are actions. According to Merriam-Webster, "way" means, "...characteristic, regular, or habitual manner or mode of being, behaving, or happenings...."[23] In Hebrew, the word is *darak*, which means to follow a well-worn path. So knowing the ways of God is to know His character and His feelings (as much as we can in this life) rather than just His actions, and to seek His face, not just His hand.

Being Conformed

"Now the length of time the Israelite people lived in Egypt was 430 years. At the end of the 430 years, to the very day, all the Lord's divisions left Egypt. Because the Lord kept vigil that night to bring them out of Egypt, on this night all the Israelites are to keep vigil to honor the Lord for the generations to come" (Exodus 12:40–42).

The Passover is one of many times in Israel's history that God showed Himself strong to His enemies that He might reveal His love and character to a faithless Israel. The Israelites had to come to a place where they knew God was working for their good. The Passover was a "suddenly" (11:1, 12:11), and the deliverance happened quickly. After the people celebrated the Passover, they bowed down and worshipped (12:27). They believed, but that belief was not yet a part of their lifestyle.

"And we know that in all things God works for the good of those who love him, who have been called according to his purpose. For those God foreknew he also predestined to be conformed to the likeness of his Son, that he might be the firstborn among many brothers. And those he predestined, he also called; those he called, he also justified; those he justified, he also glorified. What, then, shall we say in response to this? If God is for us, who can be against us?" (Romans 8:28–31).

The Israelites had to know in their heart of hearts that God loved them and was working His ways into their lives.

"Jesus Christ is the same, yesterday, today, and forever" (Hebrews 13:8). God's purposes and ways are the same, from year to year, century to century, and millennium to millennium. The Israelites had to know in their heart of hearts that God loved them and was working His ways into their lives. He wanted a people who would conform to His ways and would uniquely reflect His nature to the peoples around them, so they could be a blessing to the nations (Genesis 12:3). The same is true for each of us who follows God.

Next Stop: The Wilderness

After the Passover, God took the Israelites into the wilderness. He wanted to remove the ways of Egypt from their lives so He could teach them His ways. The people of Israel had been slaves in Egypt for 430 years. This was the only way of life they had known. When you are a slave, literally or culturally, you often cannot see beyond the next task that has to be completed. It doesn't matter whether the task is making bricks without straw, writing a paper for school or a report for work, or performing nursery duty at church. The Israelites had been complaining bitterly to God about their lot in life. Could this mean that they were in the habit of murmuring and complaining, rather than worshipping?

The direction God gave to Moses was to tell Pharaoh, *"The LORD God of the Hebrews has met with us; and now, please, let us go **three days' journey into the wilderness**, that we may sacrifice to the LORD our God"* (Exodus 3:18, emphasis added). God always intended to take them into the wilderness! It was to be a place of worship and for the sacrifice to die. It was Plan A, not Plan B.

God always intended to take them into the wilderness! It was to be a place of worship and for the sacrifice to die.

Studies have shown that it took seven years for people who were under communism to begin to think differently and freely. It is a process to unlearn one way of life and begin to walk in a new way of life. If it takes twenty-one days to learn a new habit, it makes sense that it will take longer to learn a whole new way of living. I don't know about you, but I don't change overnight, even when God gives me the heart revelation. It is especially hard if the new way of life runs counter to the way our culture or self nature drives us to live.

Grace in the Wilderness

Once in a while, God will take us through the wilderness. Ouch! We have been taught for years that we are sent to the wilderness when we do wrong: "You're going to keep going around this mountain until you get it right!" I hate to think how many times I've heard that in the church. (Perhaps more painful is the number of times I've said it to others!) The Bible **does** indicate that the wilderness **can** be a place of judgment. However, when I did a study in the scriptures on the wilderness, I found a whole different perspective. **It can be an invitation to a new way of life.**

- The people of Israel *"found grace in the wilderness"* (Jeremiah 31:2).
- The Shulamite woman came *"up from the wilderness,*

Leaning upon her beloved" (Song of Solomon 8:5).
- Hosea calls the Valley of Achor (Valley of Trouble) the Door of Hope. It is here that Israel learns to sing and declare that the Lord is her husband (Hosea 2:14–17).
- David found refuge in the wilderness strongholds in Ziph and En Gedi when he was escaping Saul (1 Samuel 23:14, 26:1–3).
- John the Baptist came out of the wilderness as *"the voice of one crying in the wilderness: 'Prepare the way of the Lord; Make His paths straight'"* (Matthew 3:3).
- Jesus came out of the wilderness (having overcome the temptations of Satan), and *"returned in the power of the Spirit"* (Luke 4:14).
- Jesus often withdrew into the wilderness to pray (Luke 5:16).
- Paul the Apostle spent three years alone in the Desert of Arabia being tutored by the Holy Spirit (rather than Apostles) and being prepared for His call (Galatians 1:16–18).

Israel's Choice

Exodus 19 and 20 describe Israel's close encounter with God. Yahweh required the people to be consecrated and declared that Mt. Sinai was holy. God appeared on the third day in the midst of thunder, lightning flashes, a thick cloud, smoke, earthquakes, and the sound of trumpets. God spoke to Moses. He set physical boundaries for the people and then gave the Ten Commandments. It was an awesome and fearsome experience. *"Now all the people witnessed the thunderings, the lightning flashes, the sound of the trumpet, and the mountain smoking; and **when the people saw it, they trembled and stood afar off.** Then they said to Moses, 'You speak with us, and we will hear; but **let not God speak with us, lest we die.'** And Moses said to the people, 'Do not fear; for **God has come to test you, and that His fear may be before you, so that you may not sin.'** So the people stood afar off, but Moses drew near the thick darkness where God was"* (Exodus 20:18–21, emphasis added). This was a personal visitation by God to the nation of Israel. It was a corporate experience that was intended to change their DNA. At this point, the nation of Israel chose not to have a direct relationship to God. A deep encounter with God filled them with fear instead of fear of the Lord. As a result they wanted an intermediary—Moses. The other intermediary was the *Torah*. Immediately after this experience, Moses went up into the thick darkness to get a further definition of the *Torah* (Exodus 20:22–23:33). *"Moses came and told the people all the words of the LORD and all the judgments. And all the people answered with one voice and said, 'All the words which the LORD has said we will do'"* (Exodus 24:3). The people ratified the covenant with blood sacrifices and verbal oaths. God then gave Moses, Aaron and two of his sons, and the seventy elders of Israel another encounter with God. *"**They saw the God of Israel.** And there was under His feet as it were a **paved work of sapphire stone,** and it was like **the very heavens in its clarity.** But on the nobles of the children of Israel He did not lay His hand. So **they saw God, and they ate and drank**"* (Exodus 24:10–11, emphasis added). The leadership of Israel was in the throne room on the sapphire pavement, seeing God, and eating and drinking. This could have been intended for the whole nation, had they not cried out for an intermediary. This is a shadow of the Wedding Feast for Jesus (the Bridegroom) and the Bride (us)!

It was God's intention to give the Ten Commandments and Torah as His teaching and instruction only until Israel came into a heart relationship and could hear His voice themselves.

God's heart is evident in Ezekiel 36:24–28: *"I will take you from among the nations, gather you out of all countries, and bring you into your own land. Then I will sprinkle clean water on you, and you shall be clean; I will cleanse you from all your filthiness and from all your idols. **I will give you a new heart and put a new spirit within you; I will take the heart of stone out of your flesh and give you a heart of flesh.** I will put My Spirit within you and **cause you to walk in My statutes, and you will keep My judgments and do them.** Then you shall dwell in the land that I gave to your fathers;*

you shall be My people, and I will be your God."

It was God's intention to give the Ten Commandments and *Torah* as His teaching and instruction **only until** Israel came into a heart relationship and could hear His voice themselves. *"Before faith came, we were kept under guard by the law, kept for the faith which would afterward be revealed. Therefore the law was our tutor to bring us to Christ, that we might be justified by faith. But after faith has come, we are no longer under a tutor"* (Galatians 3:23–25). When by faith Israel or I can hear the voice of God, then our hearts are changed so we can follow His ways willingly. When we can't hear His voice, we have hearts of stone. Then we have to follow the letter of the law to be holy, whether it is the *Torah* or church laws. Did you know the New Testament has more commandments than the Old Testament? "God then and now wants His people directly related to Him, hearing Him, responding to Him, and living from His abundant life. He has never wavered from His commitment to restore the intimate love relationship that was lost in Eden."[24] God wants us not to live from external rules but from a heart relationship to Him. Remember that God's original intention in Exodus 3:8 was that Israel would go to the wilderness and worship Him. It is sad to admit, but there are fewer distractions in the wilderness!

Refiner's Fire

The wilderness is a place where we unlearn our old ways, and God gives us the opportunity to learn to totally trust Him to bring about His purposes in our lives. The wilderness is where God takes the potential He has placed within us and brings forth the reality. My experience is that God shuts out every other distraction in our life so we can be shut in the prayer closet with Him. But it is a choice to enter (and stay) in that place.

The wilderness is where God takes the potential He has placed within us and brings forth the reality.

Jesus responded to the Pharisees that the greatest commandment in the *Torah* was Deuteronomy 6:5: *"You shall love the LORD your God with all your heart, with all your soul, and with all your strength."* God doesn't want us to intellectually **know** this command; He wants it **written in our hearts** (*yada*) so that we walk in it in every area of our lives. God wants to change us—spirit, soul, and body—into His people. He changes us from the inside out. Then we can enthusiastically respond to the heart cry of God, *"I love the Lord my God with all my heart, with all my soul, and with all my strength!"*

Life-Changing Prayer

I have always longed for a deeper relationship with God. Through circumstances in my childhood and young adulthood, I had come to a place where I didn't trust people fully. So how could I trust a God I couldn't see when the people I could see "had done me wrong"? And how could God be good and faithful if He had allowed all these horrible circumstances to happen in my life? Was He really all-powerful if He had not healed me supernaturally and not prevented people from hurting me?

In September 1995, I prayed a prayer in a group that would totally change my life. From the depth of my heart I prayed, "I want to be totally abandoned to you, God, no matter what it costs. You are worth more to me than anything else in life." Two days later, I had a car accident that totaled my car and put me in a great deal of pain. (Don't be afraid that if you pray that same prayer, God will let you have a car accident. He works in each of our lives differently!) At the time, I was an intercessory missionary with about $240 of income per month. I cried out to God, "Why didn't you protect me because I am doing your work?" Others hinted that if I was fully in the will of God, this wouldn't have happened to me. His answer was 2 Corinthians 4:7–18:

> *But we have **this treasure in jars of clay** to show that **this all-surpassing power is from God and not from us**. We are hard pressed on every side, but not crushed; **perplexed, but not in despair**; persecuted, but not abandoned; **struck down, but not destroyed**. We always carry around in our body the death of Jesus, so that the life of Jesus may also be revealed in our body. For we who are alive are always being given over to death for Jesus' sake, **so that his life may be revealed in our mortal body**. So then, death is at work in us, but life is at work in you. It is written: "I believed; therefore I have spoken." With that same spirit of faith we also believe and therefore speak, because we know that the one who raised the Lord Jesus from the dead will also raise us with Jesus and present us with you in his presence. **All this is for your benefit, so that the grace that is reaching more and***

more people may cause thanksgiving to overflow to the glory of God. Therefore we do not lose heart. Though outwardly we are wasting away, yet inwardly we are being renewed day by day. For our light and momentary troubles are achieving for us an eternal glory that far outweighs them all. So we fix our eyes not on what is seen, but on what is unseen. For what is seen is temporary, but what is unseen is eternal. (Emphasis added)

At the time, this was not a comfort! I lived on a high hill, was in great pain, had no transportation, and had to get to doctor's appointments! I felt very alone, even though I lived with a group of people. I was shut in with God so He could deal with my heart issues. How can I fix my eyes on the unseen and eternal when my here and now hurt? It is in our weakness that He can show Himself strong, but only if we let Him.

I Promised What to God?

How often do we sing songs without realizing what we are saying to God? Sometimes we sing the words by rote and don't realize what our mouth is committing to God. Occasionally it is because His presence is so close that in the emotion of the moment we respond without thinking about the cost.

For example, have you ever sung the song *Refiner's Fire* by Brian Doerksen without thinking about the implications of what you are singing?

Purify my heart
Let me be as gold and precious silver
Purify my heart
Let me be as gold, pure gold.
Refiner's fire
My heart's one desire is to be holy
Set apart for you Lord
I chose to be holy
Set apart for you my master
Ready to do your will
Purify my heart

47

Cleanse me from within and make me holy
Purify my heart
Cleanse me from my sin, deep within.[25]

The gold or silver refined in the fire represents God's divine nature being birthed in us. We are inviting God to turn up the heat and expose the impurities so He can remove the sin from our lives so we can be holy.

The Invitation

God is gracious to us. Bob Sorge states, "God often looks down at His child and says, 'I'll pretend I didn't hear you say that to me.' But once in a while, He will hear the heart cry of one of His children and will respond with 'YES! I heard that and I will answer your prayer!' "[26] Little did we know that prayer was an acceptance of God's invitation into the wilderness or the fire of affliction.

Different scripture passages talk about the refining process that God performs in our lives for His sake and His glory. But it is also so that we will know His power and character, just as God showed Himself to the Israelites during the Passover:

> *See, I have **refined you**, though not as silver; I have **tested you** in the furnace of affliction. **For my own sake, for my own sake, I do this**. How can I let myself be defamed? I will not yield my glory to another.* (Isaiah 48:10–11, emphasis added)

> *But who can endure the day of His coming? And who can stand when He appears? For **He is like a refiner's fire And like launderers' soap**. He will sit as a refiner and a purifier of silver; He will purify the sons of Levi, And **purge them as gold and silver**, That they may offer to the LORD An offering in righteousness.* (Malachi 3:2–3, emphasis added)

> *But **He knows the way that I take; When He has tested me, I shall come forth as gold. My foot has held fast to***

His steps; I have kept His way and not turned aside. I have not departed from the commandment of His lips; I have treasured the words of His mouth more than my necessary food. (Job 23:10–12, emphasis added)

It is a choice to stay in this place, though sometimes God will "encourage" us to stay by circumstances. It is important to know **who** has loving placed us in this furnace. Rebuking individual people or Satan is not going to help. God is doing it for His sake (and ours). The Father wants a bride who is worthy of His son.

Fire

"According to Genesis 3:24, the climax of creation is a sword of fire (*lahat hahereb*) placed at the east of the Garden of Eden. The only way man could get back in was to go through the fire."[27] Returning to intimacy with God requires going through the fire. The high point of God making a covenant with Abraham was when God moved between the pieces of sacrifice as a fire (Genesis 15:17). God spoke to Moses out of a flaming bush (Exodus 3:1–6). Frequently God's manifest presence is surrounded by fire: in the pillar that Israel followed, on Mt. Sinai, or in most of the throne room scenes in the Bible: *"The sight of **the glory of the LORD was like a consuming fire on the top of the mountain** in the eyes of the children of Israel"* (Exodus 24:17, emphasis added). *"Therefore, since we are receiving a kingdom which cannot be shaken, let us have grace, by which we may serve God acceptably with reverence and godly fear. **For our God is a consuming fire**"* (Hebrews 12:28–29, emphasis added).

Returning to intimacy with God requires going through the fire.

Fire is used for judgment (Sodom and Gomorrah), for cleansing (Isaiah 6 and sacrifices), or for preparation (refiner's fire). **We cannot see God's glory until we go through the fire**. In the end times, His fire will come in love and judgment. He loves us, so He will burn out everything that separates us from Him, if we will let Him.

When we encounter God's fire, we are given a choice to respond. There was a *kairos* time when a bush was burning, but was not consumed. God created this phenomenon for an audience of one, His servant Moses:

> *Now Moses was tending the flock of Jethro his father-in-law, the priest of Midian, and he led the flock to the far side of the desert and came to Horeb, the mountain of God. There the angel of **the LORD appeared to him in flames of fire from within a bush**. Moses saw that though **the bush was on fire it did not burn up**. So Moses thought, "**I will go over and see this strange sight**—why the bush does not burn up." **When the LORD saw that he had gone over to look, God called to him** from within the bush, "Moses! Moses!" And Moses said, "Here I am." "Do not come any closer," God said. "Take off your sandals, for the place where you are standing is holy ground." Then he said, "**I am** the God of your father, the God of Abraham, the God of Isaac and the God of Jacob." At this, Moses hid his face, because **he was afraid to look at God**.* (Exodus 3:1–6, emphasis added)

Moses had at least three options when he saw this burning bush:

1. **Be an ostrich.** He could have run and hid in fear because he had never seen anything like this. I don't know about you, but when I am confounded by a new concept, my first reaction is often not wanting to deal with it. I may pretend I didn't see it or put it so low on my priority list that it never sees the light of day!

2. **Be a scientist.** He could have examined all the bushes in the area to see if any others could be burned and not consumed. He might have explored the earth and sky to see if there were any other anomalies. He could have found all the natural reasons why this phenomena

was happening, but missed the real purpose for the burning bush. He might not have seen God.

3. **Be a truster**. Moses chose to turn aside from what he was doing to ask the key unspoken question: "God, what are **You** doing in this place?" By asking this question, God was able to respond. He called Moses by name and said, "Take off your shoes, for you are standing on holy ground."

Often God will appear off the beaten track to see if we will turn aside from our hiding and our exploring to seek Him. Sometimes He will play "hide and seek" to see if we will pursue Him even when it is inconvenient or against **our** principles or doctrines.

While Moses did not fully believe in himself for what God was calling him to do, he did believe in the God who was calling him.

Refining Fire

A woman called upon a silver smith and wanted to watch him refine silver.

As she watched the silver smith, he held a piece of silver over the fire and let it heat up. He explained that in refining silver, one needed to hold the silver in the middle of the fire where the flames were the hottest as to burn away all the impurities.

The woman thought about God holding us in such a hot spot—then thought again about the verse that He sits as a refiner and purifier of silver.

She asked the silver smith, if it was true that he had to sit there in front of the fire the whole time the silver was being refined. The man answered yes. He not only had to sit there holding the silver, but he had to keep his eyes on the silver the entire time it was in the fire. If the silver was left even a moment too long in the flames, it would be destroyed. The woman was silent for a moment. Then she asked the silver smith, how do you know when the silver is fully refined?

He smiled at her and answered, "Oh that's easy—when

I can see my image in it."[28]

Kay Arthur in *As Silver Refined* describes the refining process:

And the fire is the fire of His making, for through His fire our Refiner will perfect an awesome work, a divine work. He will take what is impure and make it pure. He will take what is dull and make it beautiful. He'll take what is of potential value and reveal its actual value.

He will transform us into treasure. He'll refine us in the crucible so that He can see Himself in the silver—in you and me. And so the world, as well as the principalities and powers and hosts of Satan, can behold the triumph of the Redeemer.

The fiery flames—the array of disappointing situations in our lives, from minor irritants to major tragedies—will make the difference.

Different flames, different fires will come and go. In the pressure of their heat we'll see the impurities in our lives being released and rising to the top. Then he'll skim them off, purifying us, refining us.

He'll make the fire a little hotter, causing new impurities to rise and be released, exposed for what they are. These, too, He'll lift away.

Early in our Christian lives He may see only a dim image of himself as He looks into our crucible. But as time goes on, His image becomes clearer, more lustrous, more beautiful.

And all the while, He never leaves or forsakes his treasure.

Our Refiner never leaves the crucible, never steps away from the fire.

He is always there to make sure every flame that reaches us is exactly the right temperature—not too hot!—to accomplish its work in our lives. He knows the precise temperature to maintain so we don't face more than we can bear. He tests and proves our faith, not to discredit us, but to show us how far we've come. He perfects our perseverance.[29]

**It takes faith to believe God in fiery circumstances
– to believe He will see His reflection in our lives.**

Often we believe that the temperature of our circumstances are too hot to bear. God knows better than we do what we can (and need) to walk through. Our faith and life is very precious to God while we are in and when we have come through the refiner's fire! It takes faith to believe God in fiery circumstances – to believe He will see His reflection in our lives.

> *"And to the angel of the church of the Laodiceans write, 'These things says the Amen, the Faithful and True Witness, the Beginning of the creation of God: "I know your works, that you are neither cold nor hot. I could wish you were cold or hot. So then, because you are luke-warm, and neither cold nor hot, I will vomit you out of My mouth. Because **you say, 'I am rich, have become wealthy, and have need of nothing'**—and do not know that you are wretched, miserable, poor, blind, and naked—**I counsel you to buy from Me gold refined in the fire, that you may be rich; and white garments, that you may be clothed, that the shame of your nakedness may not be revealed**; and anoint your eyes with eye salve, that you may see. **As many as I love, I rebuke and chasten. Therefore be zealous and repent.** Behold, I stand at the door and knock. If anyone hears My voice and opens the door, **I will come in to him and dine with him, and he with Me. To him who overcomes** I will grant to sit with Me on My throne, as I also overcame and sat down with My Father on His throne. He who has an ear, let him hear what the Spirit says to the churches."'"* (Revelation 3:14–22, emphasis added)

God counseled the Laodiceans to buy gold refined in the fire and white garments so they would not be ashamed. Both are very costly in God's kingdom. They require laying down our agendas so we may receive His agenda. But most of all, it requires us knowing that we are wretched, poor, naked, and blind. It is hard for many of us in America to admit this. But in God's eyes, it is true. It is not until we reach that point that God is able to restore us. He does this because He loves us! The benefits are incredible! He opens the door and dines with us and us with Him. We have intimate fellowship! I especially enjoy a quiet meal with a special friend when we can share about what is going on in our lives. It is a time to get to know one another's hearts. Then to those of us who overcome, we get to sit with *Yeshua* on the throne. He allows us to rule and reign with Him.

Vanquishing Shame

One of the impurities God wants to remove from our lives is shame. In Revelation 3:18–19, God counsels us to *"buy from Me gold refined in the fire ... that the shame of your nakedness may not be revealed."*

Merriam Webster defines "shame" as "a painful emotion caused by consciousness of guilt, short coming, or impropriety...."[30] The Bible has 154 references to "shame" in its various forms. Eighteen Hebrew and eleven Greek words describe it! Shame first was seen in the Garden of Eden: *"Then the LORD God called to Adam and said to him, 'Where are you?' So he said, 'I heard Your voice in the garden, and I was afraid because I was naked; and I hid myself'"* (Genesis 3:9–10, emphasis added). Before they sinned, they were naked and not ashamed (Genesis 2:24) because they were covered in the glory of God. Seventy Bible verses equate shame with nakedness. Shame makes us feel naked and causes us to hide. It prevents us from seeing ourselves, or letting other people see us, not to mention God. But when we sin, we need to **run to God**, not from Him.

Some of us have personality tendencies toward shame. I have had to deal with this. I often feel guilty or ashamed (turn red) when someone thinks I have done something wrong, even if I haven't. This is the enemy bringing condemnation, rather than God bringing repentance. Often if Satan can't cause us to sin, he will shame us so the effect is the same. You have no dignity and no strength to fight. All you want to do is be alone and hide. Shame has nasty tentacles that affect not only the emotions, but also the thought patterns of the mind and our will to fight. The physical body will often reflect those emotions.

*"Therefore we also, since we are surrounded by so great a cloud of witnesses, let us **lay aside every weight**, and the sin which so easily ensnares us, and let us run with endurance the race that is set before us, looking unto Jesus, the author and finisher of our faith, who **for the joy that was set before Him endured the cross, despising the shame**, and has sat down at the right hand of the throne of God"* (Hebrews 12:1–2, emphasis added). Jesus knew shame. He hung naked and falsely accused. He hated it! He set his eyes on the vision that God had ordained for Him from before the creation of the earth. He looked forward, not backward. He laid aside the weight of shame for the glory set before Him.

*"But we have **renounced the hidden things of shame**, not walking in craftiness nor handling the word of God deceitfully, but by manifestation of the truth commending ourselves to every man's conscience in the sight of God"* (2 Corinthians 4:2, emphasis added). Shame often comes from experiences in our past that no one wanted to talk about. More often than not, these are things done to us rather than by us.

How does shame attack those in the church? Sometimes people who don't know God will not understand that we follow the ways of God. Sometimes brothers and sisters will cause it by seeking to cleanse the church. Especially in prophetic circles, we shame one another out of suspicion instead of encouraging each other. God gives us discernment so we can pray, not so we can break relationships and feel "holier than thou." God loves ALL of His kids and wants to see us succeed. We must want to see our brothers and sisters succeed!

What are some of the manifestations of shame?

*Because for Your sake I have **borne reproach; Shame has covered my face**. I have become a **stranger to my brothers**, And an **alien to my mother's children**; Because zeal for Your house has eaten me up, And the reproaches of those who reproach You have fallen on me. When I **wept** and **chastened my soul with fasting**, That* *became my reproach. I also made sackcloth my garment; I became a byword to them. Those who sit in the gate speak against me, and I am the song of the drunkards. You know my reproach, my shame, and my dishonor; My adversaries are all before You. Reproach has broken my heart, And I am full of heaviness; I looked for someone to take pity, but there was none; And for comforters, but I found none.* (Psalm 69:7–12, 19–20, emphasis added)

"Do not fear, for you will not be ashamed; Neither be disgraced, for you will not be put to shame; For you will forget the shame of your youth, And will not remember the reproach of your widowhood anymore. For your Maker is your husband, The LORD of hosts is His name; And your Redeemer is the Holy One of Israel; He is called the God of the whole earth. For the LORD has called you Like a woman forsaken and grieved in spirit, Like a youthful wife when you were refused," Says your God. (Isaiah 54:4–6, emphasis added)

My dishonor is continually before me, And the shame of my face has covered me, Because of the voice of him who reproaches and reviles, Because of the enemy and the avenger. (Psalm 44:15–16, emphasis added)

Many of the manifestations are devastating: isolation, leaders speaking against you, no one to comfort you, dishonor, heaviness, disgrace, weeping, reproach, and a sense of being forsaken. Shame weighs down the countenance. The shame is always there and it feels as though it will never leave. This is from only three scripture passages! Shame is a debilitating condition that draws us down to the pit!

In Psalm 69:13–18, the Psalmist cries out for God's mercy to deliver him. He was in God's face to save him. Finally he begs God to draw near and redeem his soul from his enemies. So we must cry out to God to redeem us. Redemption is buying us back with gold. Isaiah 54 talks about embracing God as our husband as a way of forgetting reproach. It is the call to intimacy with God. In Psalm 44:7–8, the writer boasts in what God did and praises His name forever.

God wants to remove shame from us so we can be vessels of glory. Glory is the opposite of shame. Job, after all his calamities and the words of his friends, temporarily lost his crown of glory: *"He has **stripped me of my glory**, And **taken the crown** from my head"* (Job 19:9, emphasis added). It was doubly restored in the end: *"**Instead of your shame you shall have double honor**, And instead of confusion they shall **rejoice in their portion**. Therefore in their land they shall **possess double; Everlasting joy** shall be theirs"* (Isaiah 61:7, emphasis added). *"You shall **eat in plenty and be satisfied**, And **praise** the name of the LORD your God, Who has dealt wondrously with you; And **My people shall never be put to shame**. Then **you shall know that I am in the midst of Israel:** I am the LORD your God And there is no other. My people shall never be put to shame"* (Joel 2:26–27, emphasis added).

When shame is gone, we receive a crown of glory, double honor, and everlasting joy. We are able to rejoice for what we have been given, and possess double what we had before in the spirit and the natural. We are satisfied, and praise will fill our mouths. We will know the God who is in our midst and will receive a double promise from God to never be put to shame again.

How do I **choose** to vanquish unhealthy shame?

1. Wash daily with the blood of Jesus to enter into the intimacy with Him. *"Therefore, brethren, having boldness to enter the Holiest by the blood of Jesus, by a new and living way which He consecrated for us, through the veil"* (Hebrews 10:19–20).

2. Know that He has inscribed you on the palms of His hands (Isaiah 49:16). Those nail-scarred hands make intercession for you before the Father.

3. Forgive those who shamed you and move on. Don't dwell on the past. Choose to think of Jesus and not the shame. Dwell on the good plans and future God has for you (Jeremiah 29:11).

4. I must arise from the pit and put on glory! *"Arise, shine; For your light has come! And the glory of the LORD is risen upon you. For behold, the darkness shall cover the earth, And deep darkness the people; But the LORD will arise over you, And His glory will be seen upon you"* (Isaiah 60:1–2). Psalm 69 talks about a garment of shame (sackcloth). We must choose to replace it by putting on God's garment and crown of glory.

5. Let glory rather than bitterness come from the refining fire. *"Behold, I have refined you, but not as silver; I have tested you in the furnace of affliction. For My own sake, for My own sake, I will do it; For how should My name be profaned? And I will not give My glory to another"* (Isaiah 48:10–11).

6. Take nothing less than God Himself. Do not try to accomplish anything in your own strength. *"'But My people have **changed their Glory For what does not profit**. Be astonished, O heavens, at this, And be horribly afraid; Be very desolate,' says the LORD. 'For My people have committed two evils: They have forsaken Me, the fountain of living waters, And **hewn themselves cisterns—broken cisterns that can hold no water**'"* (Jeremiah 2:11–13, emphasis added).

7. Spend time in individual and corporate praise and worship. Scripture requires it, and it changes our face of shame to a face of glory. Moses' countenance was changed (Exodus 34:29–35) as was Jesus' appearance on the mountain of transfiguration (Matthew 17:1–9).

God's Inheritance

In 1998, much of the Body of Christ was excited because Israel had been a nation since 1948. Fifty years meant it was the Year of Jubilee (Leviticus 25:8–17). It is a time to reclaim lost inheritances and to be liberated from slavery. In my heart, I kept hearing God say, "I want My inheritance." He was more interested in preparing the bride for His son than in fulfilling all the "inheritances" people were claiming. His inheritance is a bride without spot or wrinkle, one in whom He can see His reflection and through whom others can see Him shine.

"The way for us to attain the great inheritance is not to be that concerned about it, but to be completely devoted to seeing our Lord receive the reward of His sacrifice. When we look at what He did for us, leaving all of the glory that He had to come to earth, living such an impoverished life as a man, and then to be so cruelly executed by the very ones He came to save, what could any of us ever do in comparison? I acknowledge that there is obviously a high calling. I also believe that those who are overly focused on it have lost their way, and lost the true vision. We can only attain by seeing Him, not ourselves. Let us pray with Paul that the eyes of our heart will be opened to see Him, His calling, and His inheritance. Only then will we see everything else clearly."[31]

Struck Down, But Not Destroyed

I will now get back to my story. God wanted to get me to a place where I would totally trust Him that nothing could come into my life without His permission. Not sickness, abandonment, unemployment, or being without a place to call my own. Not emotional pain, physical pain, the loss of a job, or a lack of money to pay the bills. Not betrayal by Christian brothers and sisters, attacks by the enemy, loss of reputation, loss of a visible ministry, or even complete weakness and weariness. I had to get to the same place as Job, who said: *"'Naked I came from my mother's womb, and naked I will depart.* **The Lord gave and the Lord has taken away**; *may the name of the Lord be praised.' In all this,* **Job did not sin by charging God with wrongdoing**" (Job 1:21–22, emphasis added).

God was removing the mindsets of the world so that I would see things from His perspective. Just as it was for the Israelites, it is a process for us. God needs to take the old ways of seeing and doing and replace them with His new ways. He wants to be proud of His inheritance. He wants others to see His reflection in each of His people.

New Definition of Success

God is less interested in **what we do for Him** than in **who we are before Him** and other people. It is unfortunate, but in our culture we measure our own success or the success of others by what they have accomplished or accumulated.

There was no visible purpose for Israel in the wilderness. They were not warring for their inheritance. God was trying to build in them a deep trust. He provided for their every need. They didn't even have to figure out where or when to go. They merely waited for the pillar of cloud or the pillar of fire to move. Then they packed up and followed it for however long it moved. When it stopped, they stopped. How hard of a program was this to follow? By all Israel's murmuring and complaining, we know it wasn't easy.

The truth is that we human beings are programmed to be "human doings." We want to have a purpose and a goal that we are heading toward. If we have no visible goal, then we and the people around us believe that we are not successful.

So how does God view success? Is it to be obedient and follow when He says follow and not wander when He is not moving? Can it be to not complain that it isn't fair when nothing visible is happening to give us worth? Is it to not murmur that your career is going nowhere fast in the world's eyes?

God's Definition of Success

Mike Bickle in the tape series *Cultivating a Heart after God*[32] speaks of the three elements of how God defines success in our lives:

1. Knowing deep down that we are loved and enjoyed by God.

2. Lovingly and willingly obeying the commands of God.

3. Establishing our identity in a loving God.

Mike believes (and I agree) that the greatest need in today's church is to understand the emotional makeup of God in our minds and hearts. The church has studied His wisdom, character, and power. We find it hard to fathom the depth of the love that God has for each of us. Apparently the first century church had the same problem! Paul wrote to the Ephesian church: *"I pray that out of his glorious riches he may **strengthen you with power** through his Spirit **in your inner being**, so that Christ may dwell in your hearts through faith. And I pray that you**, being rooted and established in love,** may have power, together with all the saints, **to grasp how wide and long and high and deep is the love of Christ,** and to know this love that surpasses knowledge—that you **may be filled to the measure of all the fullness of God"* (Ephesians 3:16–19, emphasis added). Strength or might in the inner being is so we can begin to grasp the vastness of God's love for us.

One of our temptations is to derive our identity from our circumstances, especially from what is not happening.

One of our temptations is to derive our identity from our circumstances, especially from what is not happening. We determine our own value (or the value of other people) by looking at the successes and failures in our own lives. Do you have tapes that play inside your head that say that I'll be successful when I have:

1. A handle on my life and have no issues or problems in my life.

2. A large amount of money and a certain size of house.

3. All the right relationships in my life (marriage and deep friendships), and all the right people have positively noticed me.

4. A significant ministry touching great numbers of people and nations.

5. A body that is healthy and pretty (or handsome).

All of these are secondary factors compared to knowing that God loves me! It is great to know that God loves the people in China and you. But it is critical that each of us knows that God loves **all of me**. The wilderness season drives us to God, because these secondary factors are all taken away. The question God kept asking me was, "Am I not enough for you?" I wanted to say yes, but the truth was that He wasn't. It was hard for me to admit. In fact, I felt ashamed that He wasn't. But the truth is that I wanted the secondary rewards. I asked God to heal my heart and to reorder my priorities.

"When the first commandment is seen as a task or labor, as a sacrifice, the secondary rewards often become primary to us. In other words, our main concern becomes how much anointing is on our ministry, how much money we have, the condition of our health, or the number of deep and loyal friendships we have. These secondary rewards become our primary focus when we see ourselves as making sacrifices for God. However, such rewards become secondary when Jesus is our magnificent obsession, because our highest level of purpose is fulfilled."[33]

Higher Purpose

When I worked for IBM, I had an "influential" job, a good salary, a big house, great friends, and a fulfilling ministry at my church. I had achieved the American (Christian) Dream. Yet on the inside, I had an incredible longing for something deeper, something more. I knew that I had been created for more than the American Dream. So like Mary of Bethany, I sacrificed the symbols of my success to become a missionary. Bit by bit, God would require me to give up my security in worldly "things" to become totally dependent on Him. I nobly viewed myself as having "given it all up" to follow after God. Little did I know I had given up nothing to receive everything. I was receiving the call not to missions, but to love the Lord my God with all my heart, mind, and spirit. God was calling me to the romance of the gospel!

Pruning

As I began my wilderness journey, God removed my ability to do the very things I was strong in, almost every relationship, and pretty much all of my financial resources. It was scary because I was very naked before God and the people around me. The Loving Gardener had come to prune me. I don't know if you have ever seen a grapevine that has been pruned. In Israel, the ancient vineyards cover the hills. If you observe a pruned vine, you really can't tell if it is alive or dead because all you see is the stalk. The visible fruit is gone, and even the branches and leaves from which the fruit hung are gone. The vine is naked and ugly. It really is only an old stump. One has to see the vine with loving eyes to envision the potential that is there. It takes time for the branches and the fruit to grow again. That means **waiting** for the winter season to pass so that the new growth can come forth in the spring. I'll get back to that waiting thing in another chapter! When God began pruning me, I felt like I had been punished. My comfort during this time was John 15. Jesus said that He prunes those who bear good fruit, so that they might have even more. The pruning and the pain were my reward for a job well done!

> *"I am the true vine, and my Father is the gardener. He cuts off every branch in me that bears no fruit, while **every branch that does bear fruit he prunes so that it will be even more fruitful.** You are already clean because of the word I have spoken to you. Remain in me, and I will remain in you. **No branch can bear fruit by itself; it must remain in the vine.** Neither can you bear fruit unless you remain in me. I am the vine; you are the branches. If a man remains in me and I in him, he will bear much fruit; apart from me you can do nothing. If anyone does not*

remain in me, he is like a branch that is thrown away and withers; such branches are picked up, thrown into the fire and burned. If you remain in me and my words remain in you, ask whatever you wish, and it will be given you. **This is to my Father's glory, that you bear much fruit, showing yourselves to be my disciples. As the Father has loved me, so have I loved you. Now remain in my love. If you obey my commands, you will remain in my love,** *just as I have obeyed my Father's commands and remain in his love. I have told you this so that my joy may be in you and that your joy may be complete."* (John 15:1–11, emphasis added)

The Gardener is cutting at the places where we receive our identity and satisfaction— the heart issues.

Older, more mature vines have the most potential to produce abundant fruit, but they also require the most pruning. The pruning is no longer just the outer branches, now it is close to the heart of the vine. The Gardener is cutting at the places where we receive our identity and satisfaction—the heart issues.

As I meditated on John 15, I saw the pruning in context. I was pruned so I could grow my roots even deeper into the true vine (Jesus) that I might produce more fruit that remains for God. The pruning is to cut off the extra shoots (activities) that have grown in their own strength. He was teaching me to wait and to remain in Him. It didn't matter if the snow was covering me or the wind was whipping all around me. If I remained in Him, I would once more bear fruit, even more abundantly. The question was how to remain in Him when my circumstances and my emotions were crying out to be fixed NOW! How do I remain in His love? Verse 10 says that I do this by obeying His commands, just as Jesus obeyed the Father's commands. Hmmm... How do I obey the commands just as Jesus did? I suppose by allowing God to mold His very nature into me so I begin to respond as Jesus did. Yikes! And what commands are these? I understood these to be vague scriptural principles, like being a good Christian. But could it mean something deeper? Could some of these be the "deeper" things I was searching for?

A Heart After God's

King David was one of the few who fully embraced the reality of God loving him. The Bible is full of his mistakes (sins). And they weren't little ones: adultery, murder, and disobedience. Yet God said that David was a man after His own heart (1 Samuel 13:14) because he totally embraced the love and forgiveness of God. David had passed over to that place where he was God's person and God was his God. He fulfilled God's desire although he sinned. He didn't just hear this reality. He walked it out in his life. You hear it in the Psalms. My desire is to walk out that reality in every area of my life. I believe it is yours, too, or you wouldn't be reading this book.

My heart cry has been that of King David's in Psalm 27:4–5: *"One thing I have desired of the LORD, That will I seek: That I may dwell in the house of the LORD All the days of my life, To behold the beauty of the LORD, And to inquire in His temple. For in the time of trouble He shall hide me in His pavilion; In the secret place of His tabernacle He shall hide me."* My desire is to be in full-time ministry worshipping the Lord, beholding His beauty, and asking what is on His heart to pray. He gave me that desire for eight years. But, like King David, He called me to be a full-time minister in business (a figurative King). I have had to learn how to answer the call as a senior manager, working long hours in a stressful Information Technology consulting company AND to behold His beauty as a regular priority. My reward for a job well done is to spend intimate time with God! This is the place where I am energized and rebuilt so I am able to do my kingly duties in the world. I suspect it took David time to figure it out, too. After all, he made a few mistakes himself! I am relieved that a man after God's own heart made errors of judgment and huge mistakes. It gives me great hope. The key is to learn to put first things first!

Mary of Bethany

Mary of Bethany was willing to be misunderstood by her sister and the others of her day. Mary wanted to spend time in Jesus' presence, even if the dishes didn't get done all the time. *"Now it happened as they went that He entered a certain village; and a certain woman named Martha welcomed Him into her house. And she had a sister called **Mary, who also sat at Jesus' feet and heard His word.** But **Martha was distracted with much serving,** and she approached Him and said, 'Lord, do You not care that my sister has left me to serve alone? Therefore tell her to help me.' And Jesus answered and said to her, 'Martha, Martha, you are worried and troubled about many things. But **one thing is needed,** and **Mary has chosen that good part,** which will not be taken away from her'"* (Luke 10:38–42, emphasis added).

We have forgotten that the main reason to become a Christian is to be in a relationship with Jesus not "to have a ministry."

Many Marthas in the church today are distracted with much serving. Some emphasize the importance of "being about the Kingdom's business." Often this is to the exclusion of maintaining the love relationship with God and "real" relationships with others in the Body of Christ or even their own families. Jesus' words in Mark 12:29–32 follow: *"Jesus answered him, 'The first of all the commandments is: "Hear, O Israel, the LORD our God, the LORD is one. And you shall love the LORD your God with all your heart, with all your soul, with all your mind, and with all your strength." This is the first commandment. And the second, like it, is this: "You shall love your neighbor as yourself." There is no other commandment greater than these.'"* I believe there is a real call going out from God today—to put first things first. He wants us to fall in love with Him again, to return back to our first love. We have gotten too busy with serving. We have forgotten that the main reason to become a Christian is to be in a relationship with Jesus not "to have a ministry." The priority of having a daily time with God is critical in the times we are approaching. This time should not be a laundry list, telling God what we want Him to do in the situations of our lives (or even in the lives of others). It must be a two-way conversation. God wants to share what is on His heart, not just hear what is worrying us. Have you ever had a friend who always interrupts before you tell a story, and is more interested in telling you what to do than in listening? God wants friends like Abraham, David, Moses, and Mary. They listened.

Mary of Bethany was one who truly understood who Jesus was and the price He was paying:

> *And being in Bethany at the house of Simon the leper, as He sat at the table, a woman came having **an alabaster flask of very costly oil of spikenard**. Then she broke the flask and poured it on His head. But there were some who were indignant among themselves, and said, "Why was this fragrant oil wasted? For it might have been sold for more than three hundred denarii and given to the poor." And **they criticized her sharply**. But Jesus said, "Let her alone. Why do you trouble her? **She has done a good work for Me**. For you have the poor with you always, and whenever you wish you may do them good; but Me you do not have always. She has done what she could. **She has come beforehand to anoint My body for burial**. Assuredly, I say to you, wherever this gospel is preached in the whole world, **what this woman has done will also be told as a memorial to her**."* (Mark 14:3–9, emphasis added)

"Spikenard or nard was a fragrant plant of Indian origin from which was extracted an aromatic oil, very precious and highly valued. The sweet smell of the nard is a symbol of the bride's love"[34] as in the Song of Solomon 1:12. So Mary was anointing Jesus for burial, but was also prophetically recognizing Him as the bridegroom. This extravagant, selfless act is memorialized in scripture forever. Some commentaries suggest that the alabaster flask of spikenard was her inheritance to be used as a dowry. A woman without a dowry was not likely to be asked in marriage. So she was spending her hopes for an earthly marriage in extravagant love for her heavenly bridegroom. This was truly a selfless act.

The Beloved Disciple

It has always intrigued me that John the Apostle identified himself only as the "disciple whom Jesus loved" (John 13:23). He performed miracles, saw the crucifixion and the resurrected Jesus, and had the great prophetic experience in the book of Revelation. He had come to such an understanding of Jesus' love for him that he didn't need to say "Yes, that was me, John, leaning on Jesus' breast during the last supper!" This is a change for the "Son of Thunder" who wanted to be recognized and to sit in the primo spot at Jesus' right hand! Somewhere in John's time with Jesus, he was transformed to really understand the love of Jesus. It comes through clearly in the three letters of John. I suspect that Jesus lovingly confronted him about his pride and the sin issues in his life. When he hit bottom, he was able to humbly embrace the love Jesus offered him. This changed him to the core of who he was. By coming to the end of himself, he was able to know that God loved him even in his failures. Some may think it is arrogant to admit publicly (and for all posterity) that I am "the one whom Jesus loves." But friends, that is how God wants us to be!

John had learned to lean on the breast of Jesus. He knew what it meant to have an intimate relationship with Jesus. The Shulamite woman in the Song of Solomon also learned this. In 2:16 she says, *"My beloved is mine, and I am his."* In 6:3, her focus switches from what she wants to a mutual love: *"I am my beloved's, And my beloved is mine."* In 7:10, she realizes how passionately her beloved wants her! *"I am my beloved's, And his desire is toward me."* And that is enough. It is at this point that others recognize that she has a leaning heart: *"Who is this coming up from the wilderness, Leaning upon her beloved?"* (Song of Solomon 8:5). To know how much God loves us takes a deliberate, leaning heart.

When we know we are loved, we can see others as part of the "Beloved." In the three letters of John, he calls the body of Christ "beloved" nine times. Because he knew God's love deeply, he was able to call others "beloved" despite all the things that had happened to him. He was boiled in oil by the Romans and lived to tell, only to be exiled to the Isle of Patmos! I do not discern any bitterness or anger for the way he was treated. "And so the task becomes that of allowing the blessing to touch us in our brokenness. Then our brokenness will gradually come to be seen as an opening toward the full acceptance of ourselves as the Beloved. This explains why true joy can be experienced in the midst of great suffering. It is the joy of being disciplined, purified, and pruned."[35] By believing God's love first, he was able to believe in the goodness of others. He understood the first and second commandments. He got first things first.

Being Loved in Weakness

I don't know about you, but one of the hardest things for me is to admit that I am weak. I can say that I made a mistake. I can even say that I don't know. It is tough to say that I can't do it all. Especially in the United States, we are trained to grab life with all the gusto we can or at least die trying! So we lean toward one of two tendencies. The first is that I am invincible and nothing can touch me (especially if I don't admit a problem exists). The second is to live in the place of brokenness and think it will never change.

But God. Those wonderful words, "But God." There go I, but for the grace of God. But God intervened in the situation. God never leaves us alone. Until we realize that we are not making our own opportunities, and that it is God who opens and closes doors, we can never fully be grateful. Until we realize we are weak, we don't need a savior. Until I know that MY sins required Jesus to die on the cross, I can never embrace who I really am, because I don't know who Jesus really is. I need to know that I am broken before I can believe that He can put me back together as new. We are all broken in different ways. The world, other people, evil forces, and our own choices have formed us in unique ways.

"He wants us secure in love, secure that He enjoys us in love and that our love, though weak, is still seen as genuine by God."[36] We are like Peter in John 21:15–19 who, after denying the Lord three times, needed to be restored. "Jesus was breaking the power of the shame related to Peter's failure in order to reinstate him into a position of confidence in the throne of grace. This, however, is not the only thing happening in this passage. So often when we fall and come up short, we want to shut out the grace of God. We want to put ourselves on probation or into purgatory for a season. We beat ourselves up emotionally for a while, thinking that by doing so we will somehow come to deserve forgiveness. But when we do, we are placing our confidence in something other than the finished work of the cross. If we fix our eyes and hearts on the finished work that was accomplished in His death, the Lord will then come to us and cause us to confess the truth of who we are before Him."[37] When we are in the midst of failure, we are ashamed. We can't believe that God, who knows all about our failures, actually sees us as lovers of Jesus.

I can remember in my private times with God tentatively saying, "I love You." In reality, it was more of a question: "Do You know I love You, and do You love me back?" I was locked into the recognition of my own sin and weakness. I came to God because I wanted to be loved by Him, yet I wasn't fully sure He loved me. It was a vicious circle. I had a hard time embracing the reality that I was loved by God. I was as radical for the Lord as Peter, yet there was an underlying insecurity in my heart—Did God love me constantly? Or did He love me only when I got things right? Is He a judge looking for my every mistake so He can punish me?

I have embraced the fact that God loves me passionately! Not only does He love me, but He likes me. He looks at my heart and likes what He sees in it. He sees that I want to follow him wholeheartedly, even when I stumble. This is what David did. It is what John and Peter did. I am following a well-worn path. Now when I sin, I run to my God, rather than hiding from Him in shame. *"'My grace is sufficient for you, for My strength is made perfect in weakness.' Therefore most gladly I will rather boast in my infirmities, that the power of Christ may rest upon me"* (2 Corinthians 12:9, emphasis added).

I cared for a friend's dog named Zechariah. He doesn't always get it right. He is in a new environment and barks at many new sounds. When I correct him by voice, he will sometimes run under a table in shame and fear. In fact, he lashes out in anger at me because of a previous owner's abuse. I love him. When he is afraid or ashamed, I would love to have him come running to me so I can hold him and love him. He hasn't reached that point of trust yet. I long to have that type of relationship with him. I love him for who he is, not for what he does or does not do right. I think God has been giving me a picture of how we act and what He wishes we would do!

So have you been asking for more fruitfulness and abundance in your life? Has there been a longing for the deeper things? Have you been crying to God that there must be something more than this? God is asking for your heart. Will you submit to His process for producing Christ-likeness in you?

Empowerment in the Wilderness

What is the wilderness? Scriptures use the word "wilderness" to describe a geographical area, a place of punishment, a place of preparation, a refuge from danger, and a dwelling place for evil spirits. It has positive and negative connotations. Merriam-Webster describes "wilderness" as "a tract or region uncultivated and uninhabited by human beings…"[38] Many environmentalists want to save the wilderness areas of the United States. They are viewed as the unspoiled places of the country and so are considered precious. This is also a positive connotation. So why has the wilderness gotten such a bad rap in Christian circles?

Time of Preparation

God has used the wilderness as a time of preparation for some of God's strongest deliverers: Moses, David, Joseph, Jesus, John the Baptist, and—a personal favorite—Deborah. Apparently, deliverers or forerunners need to live close to the edge to gain a dependence on God rather than on themselves. It is only when this realization happens that God is able to deliver a nation through them. *"The voice of one crying in the wilderness: 'Prepare the way of the LORD; Make straight in the desert A highway for our God.'"* (Isaiah 40:3, emphasis added, Matthew 3:3, Mark 1:3, Luke 3:4, and John 1:23). All four gospels quote this verse from Isaiah when discussing John the Baptist. That fact makes it a very significant verse. Are you in the wilderness? Perhaps God is preparing you to be a forerunner to deliver a family, a business, a church, or even a nation.

In the wilderness, God places within the depths of who you are a message (a voice) to speak at the proper time. He forms His essence in you, even if He does not tell you what you will do. God prepares a unique message for you that is built out of your personal walk with Him. *"The word of God came to John the son of Zacharias in the wilderness"* (Luke 3:2). Often we won't know what the message is until it burns within our bones. *"But His word was in my heart like a burning fire Shut up in my bones; I was weary of holding it back, And I could not"* (Jeremiah 20:9). At the *kairos* time, God will release the messenger who will then have a voice.

Moses was reluctant to speak after spending forty years in the furnace of the wilderness (Exodus 4:10–13). God told him that He would provide the words at the right time. The wilderness is not a time to develop a set of messages, but it is a time where the character is being formed and the ability to hear the voice of God is instilled deep into the person. *"Now therefore, go, and I will be with your mouth and teach you what you shall say"* (Exodus 4:12).

The wilderness is not a time to develop a set of messages, but it is a time where the character is being formed and the ability to hear the voice of God is instilled deep into the person.

Probably about five years ago, through a couple of different people, God said I would be writing a book. I was working on a prayer and research project in Colorado Springs and thought that would be the subject of my book. I contributed significantly to a book that came out of the project, but that was not my book. God had been speaking to me about trusting Him in the midst of difficult circumstances. My perception was that at any moment now I will have learned my lesson and be done with this season of my life. Little did I know! God has been building Himself in me during this time. This book is the fruit of that process. It is a very different message than I would have produced five years ago! The funny thing to me is that the more I write, the more I find of what God has placed within me to say. It is very exciting!

Transformation of the Wilderness

God loves to hide meaning in scriptures, so we will dig to pull treasure out. Let's consider the wilderness as a metaphor for what God desires to do in the life of His people whom He is preparing in the wilderness. According to the following passages in Isaiah, the wilderness (us) will be transformed:

> *Until the Spirit is poured upon us from on high, And the* **wilderness becomes a fruitful field,** *And the* **fruitful field** *is counted as a forest. Then* **justice will dwell in the wilderness,** *And* **righteousness remain in the fruitful field.** *The* **work of righteousness will be peace,** *And the effect of righteousness,* **quietness and assurance forever.** *My people will* **dwell in a peaceful habitation, In secure dwellings,** *and in* **quiet resting places.** (Isaiah 32:15–18, emphasis added)

What an awesome picture of how God wants to transform us in the wilderness season. The "desert" aspects won't be visible anymore. To summarize, God will change us:

- We will go from barrenness to being a fruitful field that becomes a forest.
- Justice, righteousness, and peace will dwell in and through us.
- Quietness and assurance will be our emotional state.
- We will dwell in peaceful, secure, and quiet habitations.

> *The wilderness and the wasteland shall be glad for them, And the* **desert shall rejoice and blossom as the rose;** *It shall* **blossom abundantly and rejoice,** *Even with* **joy and singing.** *The glory of Lebanon shall be given to it, The excellence of Carmel and Sharon.* **They shall see the glory of the LORD, The excellency of our God.** *Strengthen the weak hands, And make firm the feeble knees. Say to those*

*who are fearful-hearted, "**Be strong, do not fear!** Behold, your God will come with vengeance, With the recompense of God; He will come and save you." Then the **eyes of the blind shall be opened**, And the **ears of the deaf shall be unstopped**. Then the **lame shall leap** like a deer, And the **tongue of the dumb sing**. For **waters shall burst forth in the wilderness**, And **streams in the desert**. The parched ground shall **become a pool**, And the thirsty land springs of water; In the habitation of jackals, where each lay, There shall be grass with reeds and rushes. A highway shall be there, and a road, And **it shall be called the Highway of Holiness**. The unclean shall not pass over it, But it shall be for others. Whoever walks the road, although a fool, **Shall not go astray**. No lion shall be there, Nor shall any ravenous beast go up on it; It shall not be found there. But the **redeemed shall walk there**, And the **ransomed of the LORD shall return**, And come to Zion with singing, With **everlasting joy on their heads**. They shall **obtain joy and gladness**, And **sorrow and sighing shall flee away**.* (Isaiah 35:1–10, emphasis added)

As the wastelands in our life are transformed we will:

- Rejoice and sing, and blossom abundantly as the rose.
- See the excellency and glory of the Lord.
- Be strong and not fear.
- See and perform supernatural miracles: the blind will see, the deaf will hear, the lame will leap, and the dumb will sing.
- Experience living waters and streams flow from us.
- See the roads and rivers become paths or ways out of the wilderness.

*I will **open rivers in desolate heights**, And **fountains in the midst of the valleys**; I will make the **wilderness a pool of water**, And the dry land springs of water. I will plant in the wilderness the cedar and the acacia tree, The myrtle and the oil tree; I will set in the desert the cypress tree and* the pine And the box tree together, That **they may see and know**, And **consider and understand together**, That **the hand of the LORD has done this**, And the **Holy One of Israel has created it**. (Isaiah 41:18–20, emphasis added)

*Behold, **I will do a new thing**, Now **it shall spring forth; Shall you not know it? I will even make a road in the wilderness And rivers in the desert**. The beast of the field will honor Me, The jackals and the ostriches, Because I give waters in the wilderness And rivers in the desert, To give drink to My people, My chosen. This people I have formed for Myself; They shall declare My praise*. (Isaiah 43:19–21, emphasis added)

In the wilderness God will open up the deep places in us so that:

- We will be a pool so that thirsty humanity may drink from the depths of God within us.
- Wild animals will not attack us.
- We will be on and show the way to the Highway of Holiness so we and others will not go astray.
- Sorrow and sighing will flee away and be replaced by joy and singing.
- When people see us, they will see, know, and understand that the Lord has done this new thing in us.

*Let the wilderness and its cities **lift up their voice**, The villages that Kedar inhabits. Let the **inhabitants of Sela sing**, Let them **shout from the top of the mountains**. Let them **give glory to the LORD**, and **declare His praise** in the coastlands. The **LORD shall go forth like a mighty man; He shall stir up His zeal like a man of war. He shall cry out**, yes, shout aloud; **He shall prevail against His enemies**. I have held My peace a long time, I have been still and restrained Myself. Now I will cry like a woman in labor, I will pant and gasp at once*. (Isaiah 42:11–14, emphasis added)

For the LORD will comfort Zion, He will comfort all her waste places; He will make her wilderness like Eden, And her desert like the garden of the LORD; Joy and gladness will be found in it, Thanksgiving and the voice of melody. (Isaiah 51:3, emphasis added)

The wilderness will bring forth change in us:

- A song will be heard in our heart.
- We will lift our voices in songs and shouts, giving glory to the Lord.
- We will be like the Garden of Eden. Perfect fellowship with God will be restored.
- We will be full of thanksgiving.

In addition to changing us, God will do the following:

- Save and avenge us.
- Prevail against our enemies as a man of war.
- Comfort Zion.

What an awesome transformation God will work in my life and yours when we submit to the wilderness experience!

Today the nation of Israel is a prophetic example of this. In 1948, not a single tree stood in the nation because the people had been taxed on the number of trees on their properties. Today much of the land has been transformed from desert to lush and green farmland. It produces magnificent flowers and fruits that are sent all over the world. Her borders are not secure, nor is the nation a peaceful habitation. But God is not finished with her yet.

I know God has not finished transforming me either. I don't reflect all these characteristics, and yet I hope that God will complete that which He has begun. I recognize I am not the same person I was ten years ago. If I had not gone through the wilderness experiences, I would not be where I am in God today. Some of those experiences were by my choice, and some were by God's choice. I have made the decision to believe that God is greater than the circumstances in my life. **Nothing** can touch my life without

His permission. Therefore, He will give me the grace to walk it through.

I have made the decision to believe that God is greater than the circumstances in my life. Nothing can touch my life without His permission.

Let me encourage you to stay in the situation God places you until He releases you to move on.

Wrestling with God

*Then **Jacob was left alone; and a Man wrestled with him until the breaking of day**. Now when He saw that He did not prevail against him, He touched the socket of his hip; and the socket of Jacob's hip was out of joint as He wrestled with him. And He said, "Let Me go, for the day breaks." But he said, "**I will not let You go unless You bless me!**" So He said to him, "What is your name?" He said, "Jacob." And He said, "Your name shall no longer be called Jacob, but Israel; for **you have struggled with God and with men, and have prevailed**." Then Jacob asked, saying, "**Tell me Your name, I pray.**" And He said, "Why is it that you ask about My name?" And **He blessed him there**. So Jacob called the name of the place **Peniel: "For I have seen God face to face**, and my life is preserved." Just as he crossed over Penuel the sun rose on him, and he limped on his hip. (Genesis 32:24–31, emphasis added)*

Jacob was running in fear from Esau. A Man (most scholars agree this was a pre-incarnate visit of *Yeshua*) stopped him in his tracks. They wrestled all night. Jacob's hip was placed out of socket and he was in great pain, yet he would not give up. In his heart he knew it was God. "I will not let you go until you bless me!" How many of us, when the pain in our lives becomes intense, give up before God blesses us? Perseverance is key in the midst of our struggles. Note Jacob did not wrestle with himself or other people. He wrestled in the face of God. We must always run to God in the midst of our pain. It is when we are able to see God face to face in the midst of the pain that we begin to see our identities change. Jacob, the deceiver, was changed into Israel, meaning he will rule as God. The blessing is meant to be the end of the season of wrestling.

Not long before this encounter, Jacob had reminded God of His promises (32:12). In the hard times, this is important because it builds our faith. In Biblical terms, our names reveal who we are, our character. God required Jacob to admit his true nature (32:27) before he could be changed. Whatever name you believe you have negatively been called, God wants to change it to how He sees you. God wants us to be so transformed by the wrestling process that we lose our old identities. We are transformed into His identity and nature.

Are you wrestling with God? Or are you turning your back on Him because you think your life stinks? Tell Him what you think. He can take it. But don't turn your back on Him.

Wise Virgin Call

The primary call of the wilderness time is to produce oil in your lamp. Developing your private walk with God is the key to transformation in the wilderness:

> *"Then the kingdom of heaven shall be likened to ten virgins who took their lamps and went out to **meet the bridegroom**. Now five of them were wise, and five were foolish. Those who were **foolish took their lamps and took no oil** with them, but the **wise took oil in their vessels with their lamps**. But while the bridegroom was delayed, they all slumbered and slept. And at midnight a cry was heard: 'Behold, the bridegroom is coming; go out to meet him!' Then **all those virgins arose and trimmed their lamps**. And the foolish said to the wise, '**Give us some of your oil, for our lamps are going out**.' But the wise answered, saying, '**No, lest there should not be enough for us and you**; but go rather to those who sell, and **buy for yourselves**.' And while they went to buy, the*

*bridegroom came, and **those who were ready went in
with him to the wedding;** and the door was shut.
Afterward the other virgins came also, saying, 'Lord,
Lord, open to us!' But he answered and said, 'Assuredly, I
say to you, **I do not know you.' Watch therefore**, for you
know neither the day nor the hour in which the Son of
Man is coming."* (Matthew 25:1–13, emphasis added)

To properly understand this parable, let's examine the process of
producing olive oil. It takes approximately fifteen years for an olive
tree to begin to produce oil (revelation). Once a tree produces, it
will continue for three to four hundred years. In Israel, there are
trees in the Church of All Nations, near the Garden of Gethsemane,
that were growing in Jesus' time. Olive trees grow in rocky, barren
areas—a wilderness. Oil comes out of staying in the hard place, but
the results can last for long periods of time. Have you noticed how
difficult it is to remove oil from clothes or tablecloths? In Hebrew,
"Gethsemane" (*gat shemmen*) means the pressing of olive oil. Jesus
went to the oil press to prepare for the cross. The disciples were
asleep like the above virgins. Every revelation costs something.
Gethsemane cost Jesus His very life.

What happens to the olive? The flesh of the olive is crushed.
Three grades of oil are produced. The first pressing or "beaten oil"
is from beating the olives and placing them in wicker baskets for
the oil to run out. This is the lightest and highest grade oil. Crushing
the olives in the oil press produces the next grade of oil. Lastly, the
olives are heated to remove the last bit of oil from the pulp, which is
the final grade of oil. Oil was used for ordinary life functions such
as cooking, skin care, lamps, and the healing of wounds. It was also
used for sacred functions such as a base for anointing oil or was
offered in worship.[39] When God places you into His oil press, all
the desires, attitudes, habits that do not reflect God are crushed.
Like Jesus, your will is submitted to God's will (Luke 22:42). It is
one of the most difficult and painful places. While it may look like
you are depressed, it is really that you are being pressed out.

All ten are virgins—representing the redeemed. The difference
was how much oil the five wise and the five foolish virgins had. We
"buy" or pay the price for oil by reading the word of God, worship-

ping, spending time with Jesus in prayer, and keeping right heart attitudes. The wise virgins knew that they could not do this for the foolish virgins. It is a personal discipline to keep up our oil supply. The wise virgins refused to give their oil to the foolish virgins. On first reading, this looks selfish and "unchristian." But the wise virgins realized that each individual needs to develop a personal history with God in the secret place where no one else goes. The fruit of the secret times (the light in the lamp) can be shared at times. But the oil (our own relationship with God) that lights the lamp (ministry) cannot be shared. The wise virgins told the foolish virgins **where** they could buy oil. The wise virgins realized that they did not know how much oil they needed to be ready for the approach of the bridegroom. Each of us must constantly renew our supply of oil and know when to expend it in the lamp. When the bridal party arrived, those that were ready went in and the door was shut. There is a season for developing oil, but it is not forever. We need to be watchful and faithful to be ready for the approaching wedding. What's most scary is that the Lord said He didn't **know** the foolish virgins (redeemed) who didn't have enough oil. I want to be one who is ready, one who is known by Jesus. How about you?

I have had seasons in which I had to learn to receive from the Lord and then to keep silent. Through some mistakes, I learned that God requires a message to mature before it is delivered. God longs to give us a revelation. But He wants us to learn to chew on it and live it before we are to teach it. We need to walk it out. This is how we develop "a voice" with authority.

He does not want us to be the "answer woman" or "answer man." I mentored some ladies in intercession and intimacy with the Lord. My teaching style is now to *midrash*. Instead of imparting knowledge Western style, Rabbis taught the scriptures by *midrash,* asking key questions that draw the answers out of the students. I think it is much more fun and stimulating! But the time would always come when they would not know the answer. I learned to respond with, "What is the Lord saying to you?" instead of providing an answer. My pride wanted to give the answer! Instead, He wants me to point them to Him, so He can impart the knowledge the same as He did for me. I am an encourager and a coach on how to get oil.

A Generation Needing Deliverance

The Bible in general, and Judges in particular, is a book about revival. God's people fall away, God raises up a deliverer, the people repent, and God restores them. We are a generation needing revival. We will look at Judges chapters 4 and 5 when Deborah arose to see parallels to our times.

> *When Ehud was dead, the children of **Israel again did evil** in the sight of the LORD. So the LORD **sold them into the hand of Jabin king of Canaan**, who reigned in Hazor. The commander of his army was Sisera, who dwelt in Harosheth Hagoyim. And the children of Israel cried out to the LORD; for Jabin had nine hundred chariots of iron, and for twenty years **he harshly oppressed** the children of Israel.* (Judges 4:1–3, emphasis added)

> *In the days of Jael, The **highways were deserted**, And the travelers walked along the byways. **Village life ceased**, it ceased in Israel, Until I, **Deborah, arose, Arose a mother in Israel**. They **chose new gods**; Then there was **war in the gates**; Not a shield or spear was seen among forty thousand in Israel.* (Judges 5:6–8, emphasis added)

Today, in the year 2002, the United States (and much of the civilized world) is at war with terrorism. I can't think of a better example of lawlessness than terrorism. Tamara Winslow quotes *Strong's Concordance* to define the mystery of lawlessness (*anomia* in Greek) as:

1. A lifestyle, a mindset, or an atmosphere without rules or laws.

2. A depiction of an environment in which there are no rules or law.

3. The mystery of lawlessness gradually and subtly enforcing a mindset in which the borders of right and wrong become non-existent.

4. The truth becoming entirely relative, left to personal interpretation.

5. Doctrinal truths and boundaries being considered unimportant.

6. Experience being embraced before Biblical reality.

7. Sin being no longer defined and becoming a matter of personal preference. *"In those days there was no king in Israel; everyone did what was right in his own eyes."* (Judges 17:6)[40]

   The mystery of lawlessness is in direct opposition to God's righteousness. *"For what fellowship has righteousness with lawlessness? And what communion has light with darkness?"* (2 Corinthians 6:14). But perhaps more importantly, it is tied to our passion for God in the end times. *"And because lawlessness will abound, **the love of many will grow cold**. But he who endures to the end shall be saved. And this gospel of the kingdom will be preached in all the world as a witness to all the nations, and then the end will come"* (Matthew 24:12–14). We need to keep our passion for God fiery hot, even through difficult circumstances.

   There are many degrees of lawlessness. 1 John 3:4 states, *"Whoever commits sin also commits lawlessness, and sin is lawlessness."* This means we each have some degree of lawlessness that fights against the righteousness of God in us. It is this increase of lawlessness worldwide that sets the stage for the Anti-Christ. *"For the **mystery of lawlessness is already at work**; only He who now restrains will do so until He is taken out of the way. And then the lawless one will be revealed, whom the Lord will consume with the breath of His mouth and destroy with the brightness of His coming. The **coming of the lawless one is according to the working of Satan, with all power, signs, and lying wonders, and with all unrighteous deception among those who perish, because they did not receive the love of the truth**, that they might be saved. And for this reason God will send them strong delusion, that they should believe the lie, that they all may be condemned who did not believe* *the truth but had **pleasure in unrighteousness**"* (2 Thessalonians 2:7–12, emphasis added). One of the weapons against lawlessness is a love of the truth, who is Jesus. The greatest sin of the Israelites in Judges was idolatry—they chose other gods.

In the midst of the lawlessness in Israel, God chose Deborah to arise. "She was in a position of rulership before she assumed the position of deliverer. Her rulership and authority had been established by God—not because of anything she did. It was established because of who she was in God. A forerunner is not someone who is recognized because he or she began a great revival. A forerunner is recognized because of his or her lifestyle, his or her position in God—the revival comes as a product of the lifestyle."[41] Again, this is a call to be prepared for in our lifestyle choices, so we can arise when God calls us to a new task. He is looking for us to arise for such a time as this and He doesn't care if you are a man or a woman. He is looking for a willing heart.

God is looking over the earth to see who will be prepared to be forerunners in this hour. They will be prepared with lifestyles that reflect God. God will fill their mouths with relevant messages that will speak to hearts.

The Secret Place

> *"But you, when you pray, go into your room, and when you have **shut your door**, pray to **your Father who is in the secret place**; and your Father who sees in secret will reward you openly"* (Matthew 6:6, emphasis added).

> *"But without faith it is impossible to please Him, for he who comes to God must believe that He is, and that He is a rewarder of those who diligently seek Him"* (Hebrews 11:6).

God is sending out an invitation to come to the secret place. Why? The Father is in the secret place! He is waiting for you to come and join Him.

What else does God say about the secret place?

- Song of Solomon 2:14: "*O my dove, in the clefts of the rock, In the secret places of the cliff, Let me see your face, Let me hear your voice; For your voice is sweet, And your face is lovely.*" God calls us because He wants to see our faces and hear our voices! He desires to be with us.

- Isaiah 45:3: "*I will give you the treasures of darkness And hidden riches of secret places, That you may know that I, the LORD, Who call you by your name, Am the God of Israel.*" He calls us by our names in the secret place. He wants us to know that He is I AM, the God of Israel. Then He wants to tell us the treasures of His heart that He has hidden for us to dig up in His word.

- Zephaniah 3:14–17: "*Sing, O daughter of Zion! Shout, O Israel! Be glad and rejoice with all your heart, O daughter of Jerusalem! The LORD has taken away your judgments, He has cast out your enemy. The King of Israel, the LORD, is in your midst; You shall see disaster no more. In that day it shall be said to Jerusalem: 'Do not fear; Zion, let not your hands be weak. The LORD your God in your midst, the Mighty One, will save; He will rejoice over you with gladness, He will quiet you with His love, He will rejoice over you with singing.'*" In the secret place, God rejoices and sings over us and quiets us with His love! He takes away our judgments as we repent. He casts out our enemies. He removes our fears and weaknesses. So we should sing, shout, be glad, and rejoice with all our hearts!

- Psalm 32:6–7: "*For this cause everyone who is godly shall pray to You In a time when You may be found; Surely in a flood of great waters They shall not come near him. You are my hiding place; You shall preserve me from trouble; You shall surround me with songs of deliverance.*" He preserves us from trouble and surrounds us with songs of deliverance so that the destructive voices of the world, of other people, or even within us are drowned out.

- Isaiah 48:17–18: "*Thus says the LORD, your Redeemer, The*

Holy One of Israel: 'I am the LORD your God, Who teaches you to profit, Who leads you by the way you should go. Oh, that you had heeded My commandments! Then your peace would have been like a river, And your righteousness like the waves of the sea.'" In the secret place He teaches us what is to our benefit, and leads us in the way we should go. When we obey His word, then we have life-giving rivers of peace and vast oceans of righteousness.

• Psalm 81:7: *"You called in trouble, and I delivered you; I answered you in the secret place of thunder; I tested you at the waters of Meribah."* There is thunder in the secret place. Thunder surrounds the throne of God. Meribah means contention. God will test us with contention and then deliver us. We are to be overcomers.

• Isaiah 4:5–6: *"Then the Lord will create over all of Mount Zion and over those who assemble there a cloud of smoke by day and a glow of flaming fire by night; over all the glory will be a canopy. It will be a shelter and shade from the heat of the day, and a refuge and hiding place from the storm and rain."* The hiding place is where we dwell. We find safety when we **live** there, rather than occasionally **visit**. His glory may be seen in various forms in the hiding place. His glory will be a shelter from the storms around us.

• Isaiah 49:2: *"And He has made My mouth like a sharp sword; In the shadow of His hand He has hidden Me, And made Me a polished shaft; In His quiver He has hidden Me."* We are hidden under the shadow of His hand as He prepares a message in us to be an arrow to go after the enemy.

• Jeremiah 23:24: *" 'Can anyone hide himself in secret places, So I shall not see him?' says the LORD; 'Do I not fill heaven and earth?' says the LORD."* No one can hide from God in the secret place (or anywhere else).

• Psalm 57:1–3: *"Be merciful to me, O God, be merciful to me!*

*For **my soul trusts in You;** And **in the shadow of Your wings I will make my refuge, Until these calamities have passed by.** I will cry out to God Most High, To God who performs all things for me. He shall send from heaven and save me; **He reproaches the one who would swallow me up**"* (emphasis added). It is the place where our soul begins to trust God completely even in the midst of calamities and reproaches.

Many scriptures speak about hiding ourselves in God away from our enemies, in all the many forms. This will be critical in the days of lawlessness or terrorism. Some of the benefits are highlighted below:

- Proverbs 22:3: "***A prudent man foresees evil and hides himself,*** *But the simple pass on and are punished.*" We need to know (*yada*) that God is a safe place.

- Psalm 27:5–6: "*For **in the time of trouble He shall hide me in His pavilion; In the secret place of His tabernacle He shall hide me; He shall set me high upon a rock.** And now my head shall be lifted up above my enemies all around me; Therefore I will offer sacrifices of joy in His tabernacle.*"

- Psalm 31:19–20: "*Oh, **how great is Your goodness, Which You have laid up for those who fear You,** Which You have prepared for those who trust in You In the presence of the sons of men! You shall **hide them in the secret place of Your presence From the plots of man;** You shall keep them **secretly in a pavilion From the strife of tongues.**"

- Psalm 91:1–4: "*He who **dwells in the secret place** of the Most High Shall abide **under the shadow of the Almighty.** I will say of the LORD, 'He is my refuge and my fortress; My God, in Him I will trust.' Surely **He shall deliver you from the snare of the fowler And from the perilous pestilence.** He shall cover you with His feathers, And under His wings you shall take refuge; **His truth shall be your shield and buckler**"* (emphasis added).

I wonder if the secret place is near the throne of God. Some aspects of the description seem similar to those of the throne room, such as the sapphire pavement and thunder.

Learning to live in the secret place has been a pleasure. I used to feel like the enemy could claw my back at unexpected moments. I had my armor on, but the breastplate covered only my front. So how could I protect my back? I have learned to run to my God, my refuge in the midst of the storm. He is the eye of the hurricane where it is peaceful, while the winds blow around me. He is the lighthouse that sends a beacon showing the way home. He is the covering over me that makes me invisible to the enemy.

When I go to the secret place, it is a different experience each time. Sometimes it feels as though I am sitting in the security of my Papa's lap. Sometimes I am leaning on the breast of my beloved to be renewed. Sometimes it is the light bulb going on as I read the scriptures. Sometimes it is loud and intense prayer for a situation in my nation or another nation. Sometimes we are just talking as close friends. Sometimes myriad people float in my mind to pray for. Sometimes it is weeping over my sins or the sins of my nation. I believe variety is the spice of life. God knows that, so He comes to me in many different ways. I love it!

Time in the secret place is not wasted; it is time well spent on our relationship with God.

God loves it when we take time from our busy schedules and choose to spend time with Him. It shows our priorities. We always allocate time to what we are passionate about it, even if it is boring TV. Time in the secret place is not wasted; it is time well spent on our relationship with God. Every relationship, whether spouse, friend, or family, takes time and energy to maintain and grow. He is worth it. Your bridegroom awaits you! He is calling you to the romance of the gospel. Chris DuPre's "Dance With Me" is a description of God's invitation to dance with Him to the Song of all Songs. It is an invitation to the romance of the Gospel.

Job—Oh No, Not Him!

I can't say Job is one of my favorite books, though I have spent some time meditating on it! I chose my Freshman Seminar at Trinity College based on friends recommending a particular professor. I was excited that he would be leading a Freshman Seminar that year. Then I groaned—it was on the book of Job! I remember we read Elie Wiesel's book on his experiences during the Holocaust. We set up a courtroom reenactment in class. I don't remember what I wrote in my papers, which is probably a good thing. My ideas would be very different now, probably a lot less self-righteous! I also do not feel the need to defend God anymore.

Although the authorship of Job is unclear, many scholars believe that it was the first book of the Bible written. Scripture attests that Job was a real person who lived. Ezekiel 14:14 and James 5:11 refer to him. He was a very wealthy gentile man who knew God by the name of "Shaddai"—the Almighty. Since this is the first book written, Job lays the foundation for the rest of scripture revelation. Yet how often we ignore or misunderstand this book! It doesn't fit our paradigm of God. Hmmm…

The book of Job begins with God bragging about Job to Satan. It ends with Satan losing his bet that Job loves God only because of the blessings. I expect he didn't realize Job would be totally transformed by the process! Just like Satan didn't know that He lost when Jesus was crucified, only to be resurrected. The death process in God brings transformation. The central theme of Job is transformation.

God wants to change our paradigm of Him.

One of the fundamental truths to this book is that Job was *"blameless and upright, and one who feared God and shunned evil"* (1:1). He did nothing sinful to deserve losing his children, house, possessions, livestock, and health. Generally we want to defend God and blame Job. Somehow that fits our paradigm of God better. The calamities happened because God was bragging on Job to Satan and the angels. Satan essentially accused God of not getting it right and wanted to prove it. God gave Satan permission to "have at" Job, but (and this is important) God set the boundaries of how far Satan could go. It is critical for us to know that God is in control and **nothing** can touch us without His permission. God wants to change our paradigm of Him. *"**Who shall separate us from the love of Christ? Shall tribulation, or distress, or persecution, or famine, or nakedness, or peril, or sword?** As it is written: 'For Your sake we are killed all day long; We are accounted as sheep for the slaughter.' Yet in all these things **we are more than conquerors through Him who loved us.** For I am persuaded that **neither death nor life**, nor angels nor principalities nor powers, **nor things present nor things to come**, nor height nor depth, nor any other created thing, shall be able to **separate us from the love of God which is in Christ Jesus our Lord"** (Romans 8:35–39, emphasis added). The bottom line is that no person or thing (present or future) can separate us from the love of God. That's a pretty awesome promise. But do you believe it?

Many themes and revelations can be gleaned from the book of Job. I will choose just a few to discuss here.

The Words of Friends

Job had three friends. They cared about Job and were moved by his great cries of grief in chapter 3. They shared with him their thoughts on why this happened and what to do about it. The dialogs between Job and his three friends are recorded starting in chapter 2 verse 11 all the way through chapter 31. His friends gave very Biblical advice, but the truth is that they didn't understand Job's situation at all. They said that Job's circumstances were the result of sin, otherwise God wouldn't let this happen. They claimed to have a divine revelation from God on his circumstances. They believed Job was being self-righteous by his insistence on his integrity. "For Job, integrity refers to an uprightness of heart which purposes to follow righteousness and turn from evil. Integrity maintains a pure conscience through prompt repentance and godly behavior—to the best of one's knowledge."[42] God rebuked the three friends in 42:7–8. In fact, His wrath was aroused against them. He required them to make sacrifices and asked Job to pray for them. Elihu picked up where the others left off. He spoke for six chapters. God did not rebuke him in the end, but neither did He commend him.

Desperation

Have you ever been grieving and wanted to just spend a quiet time with a friend? To not have the person try to explain your pain away or tell you to just get over it? When we see our brothers and sisters in trying circumstances, we need to be silent and not judge, lest we be judged. One of my hardest experiences was when a friend did not understand why a transition in my life was not going smoothly. She judged by her past experience, and asked me to step down from a position. My relationship with God was vibrant and growing rapidly. I knew this transition was from God and not the enemy. Yet, I couldn't explain what was happening—the heavens were as brass. Like all people, I had sin in my life, but it was not gross immorality. I repented over everything I could think of and then some! I was in the dark and hurting. I think my gut-level honesty scared her. I wasn't going to cover up my circumstances by using trite Christian sayings. God wants us to press into Him and Him alone, without understanding our circumstances. I had to learn to pray without accusing Him or my friends! I was desperate to know Him, whatever the cost.

When God makes you desperate for Him, all the rules change. Your life is totally out of your control; you have radically different values; you don't care what others think of you; you become extremely focused on your goal; relationships take a secondary role to your own pursuit; you will take great risks because you have nothing to lose; if anyone tries to stop you, you run over them. You're desperate.

Job's friends don't know what to do with this desperate man. He's different, and they don't understand the changes. He is nothing like the Job they once knew. They're saying to each other, "We can't talk to this guy; we can't reason with him; he won't receive anything from us. What's wrong with him? Does he think we are all wrong and he's all right?" So they have no idea what to do with this man who was once their friend but now seems to be living on another planet. They don't fully understand that their friend is now a desperate man.

Take it from me: When you get thrown into a desperate pursuit of God, all your relationships change.[43]

This was my experience as well.

Fullness of Time

Job didn't know why he was struck by so many calamities. He wasn't privy to the drama played out in heaven. He just experienced the results of it on the earth. He really didn't know **why** this happened. He simply had to wait for God to speak or act. It was a matter of waiting for God's time.

In my story above, I asked several mature believers who hear the voice of God to pray over my circumstances. None had insight into what was happening, except to affirm it was from God. This is often part of the wilderness experience. While God wanted to teach me to wait on Him, He directed me to do some word studies on the various words.

The Hebrew word for **wait (and hope)** is *qavah*. The root means to wait or to look for with eager expectation. "Waiting with steadfast faith endurance is a great expression of faith. It means enduring patiently in confident hope that God will decisively act for the salvation of his people (Genesis 49:18). Waiting involves the very essence of a person's being, his soul (Psalm 130:5). Those who wait in true faith are renewed in strength so that they can continue to serve the Lord while waiting for his saving work (Isaiah 40:31).

There will come a time when all God has promised will be realized and fulfilled (Isaiah 49:23; Psalm 37:9). In the meantime, the believer survives by means of his integrity and uprightness, as he trusts in God's grace and power (Psalm 25:21). His faith is strengthened through his testings, and his character is further developed (Psalm 27:14)."[44] The quote on the cover of a church bulletin spoke to my heart: "The true believers are the unwearied waiters." I framed it so the picture is "floating" in a matte of glass with a simple wood frame. The glass represents believing in the unseen. Lord, help me wait in hope!

The Hebrew word for **renew** (*chalaph*) means to "pass on, or away, pass through, change garments."[45] It is also used in the context of Job 14:7–9, 13–14 where Job is looking for God to provide a second growth: *"For there is **hope for a tree**, if it is cut down, that it will **sprout again**, And that its tender shoots will not cease. Though its root may grow old in the earth, And its stump may die in the ground, **Yet at the scent of water it will bud** And bring forth branches like a plant. Oh, that You would **hide me** in the grave, That You would **conceal me until Your wrath is past**, That You would **appoint me a set time**, and remember me! If a man dies, shall he live again? All the days of my hard service **I will wait, Till my change comes"** (emphasis added). This sounds a lot like John 15. Lord, let me wait in hope that you will renew me!

Kairos is one of the Greek words for time or season in the New Testament. The main meaning is "a decisive point in place, situation, or time." In the Bible, it stresses "a divinely ordained appointment." "Jesus' own life stands under the claim of the kairos. He discerns the moment and decides accordingly (John 7:6,8). This kairos is not just a favorable opportunity. Jesus awaits it from the Father and thus enjoys true certainty. His end especially stands under the kairos. He himself says when it has come (Matthew 26:18), but only as he sees and grasps and accepts the kairos that is given by God. It is thus the 'right time' (Romans 5:6)."[46] 2 Timothy 4:2 uses *kairos* as in season and out of season: *"Preach the word! Be ready in season and out of season. Convince, rebuke, exhort, with all longsuffering and teaching."* Lord, let me wait in hope that you will renew me at the *kairos* time!

Waiting

Waiting has never been one of my better qualities! Perhaps that is why God gave me Isaiah 40:29–31 as one of my life verses: *"He gives power to the weak, And to those who have no might He increases strength. Even the youths shall faint and be weary, And the young men shall utterly fall, But those who wait on the LORD Shall renew their strength; They shall mount up with wings like eagles, They shall run and not be weary, They shall walk and not faint."* Part of the call in the wilderness is to "wait."

The wilderness season is doing what God puts before you, but not much else. He may show you things to do in the future, but they must first mature into a full-bodied wine. God will serve no wine (even new wine) before its time or before the wineskin has been prepared. He knows that if we saw the whole picture of what He was going to do in us and through us, we would back off in disbelief or walk in pride.

The New Testament church was born in waiting. Part of Jesus' last instruction was, *"Behold, I send the Promise of My Father upon you; but **tarry in the city of Jerusalem until** you are endued with power from on high"* (Luke 24:49, emphasis added). The story in Acts 2 is the result of that corporate waiting in the Upper Room: *"When the Day of Pentecost had fully come, they were all with one accord in one place. And suddenly there came a sound from heaven, as of a rushing mighty wind, and it filled the whole house where they were sitting. Then there appeared to them divided tongues, as of fire, and one sat upon each of them. And they were all filled with the Holy Spirit and began to speak with other tongues, as the Spirit gave them utterance"* (Acts 2:1–4).

Some years ago, I had a vision of the throne room. It was different than most visions. I was seeing the throne room in fabrics! God showed me a wall hanging that I would create. The fabrics were all expensive and gorgeous. I had no money, but I went and priced them in faith. I didn't feel a release from God to start, so I put the task on the back burner. I now have a job that pays well. God revived the vision recently. I have bought the fabrics and know this is one of my projects for the next few months. This is another example of God enriching a concept over time. If I had started it five years ago, it would not have the depth that I hope it will have. I have studied scriptures about the throne room in more detail. The picture is still evolving in my mind's eye as I pray. I am excited to see what the final picture will be like! I also pray that God will give me the right skills to craft what I am envisioning!

Hope

The Hebrew word for hope is *tiqvah*. It is the same root as "wait." It means to entwine yourself around God as a cord consisting of many strands. The word "hope" appears sixteen times in the book of Job. Hmmm... this seems to be major theme.

Many years ago, Phil Keaggy sang a song called "Disappointment—His Appointment." Much of God's challenge to me has been to wait in hope and not in disappointment. I have great expectations in God, but they always seemed to be dashed by circumstances. The Psalms talk twenty-one times about placing our hope **in** God, His mercy, or His word. Our hope is not to be in our expectation of what we think might happen (good or bad), but in God Himself.

Hope is described in the Bible as:

- **A door**: "*I will give her vineyards from there, And the Valley of Achor as a door of hope; She shall sing there, As in the days of her youth, As in the day when she came up from the land of Egypt*" (Hosea 2:15).
- **An anchor**: "*By two immutable things, in which it is impossible for God to lie, we might have strong consolation, who have fled for refuge to lay hold of the hope set before us. This hope we have as an anchor of the soul, both sure and steadfast, and which enters the Presence behind the veil*" (Hebrews 6:18–19).
- **A helmet**: "*But let us who are of the day be sober, putting on the breastplate of faith and love, and as a helmet the hope of salvation*" (1 Thessalonians 5:8).

If we are the bride of Christ in love with the bridegroom, we should live in hope. Hope is a learned behavior. It will open the door to new possibilities. Our life will be anchored in God. Our thoughts about God and ourselves will be protected.

Reality of God in the Promise

Romans 4:13–23 discusses Abraham's hope, faith, and belief in spite of what was visible in the natural realm. Abraham believed that God was able to fulfill the promise of his name, which means the father of many nations. Can you imagine going through life saying, "Hi, my name is the father of many nations"? "So how many children do you have?" "Uhm, well, uhm—none." Yet Romans 4:20 clearly says that Abraham did not waver in unbelief. This amazes me! In my mind, Abraham and Sarah wavered in unbelief numerous times. After all, isn't Ishmael the fruit of unbelief? Yet God sees Abraham through the lens of faith, and says he didn't waver in unbelief. That sure gives me hope! Abraham did this by believing in the God who calls things that do not exist as though they do. He had hope and faith that God would fulfill the promise:

> *Therefore **it is of faith** that it might be according to grace, so that the promise might be sure to all the seed, not only to those who are of the law, but also to those who are of the faith of Abraham, who is the father of us all (as it is written, "I have made you a father of many nations") in the presence of Him whom he believed—God, who gives life to the dead and **calls those things which do not exist as though they did;** who, **contrary to hope, in hope believed,** so that he became the father of many nations, according to what was spoken, "So shall your descendants be." And **not being weak in faith,** he did not consider his own body, already dead (since he was about a hundred years old), and the deadness of Sarah's womb. **He did not waver at the promise of God through unbelief,** but was **strengthened in faith, giving glory to God,** and being **fully convinced that what He had promised He was also able to perform.** And therefore "it was accounted to him for righteousness." (Romans 4:16–22, emphasis added)*

Hope in the soul realm (emotions) is what activates and strengthens faith in the spirit realm.

Hope in the soul realm (emotions) is what activates and strengthens faith in the spirit realm. *"Now **faith is the substance of things hoped for**, the evidence of things not seen. For by it the elders obtained a good testimony. By faith we understand that the worlds were framed by the word of God, so that the things which are seen were not made of things which are visible"* (Hebrews 11:1–3, emphasis added). Hope is what will bring stability to our souls when we don't know what will happen. *For **I know the thoughts that I think toward you**, says the LORD, thoughts of peace and not of evil, **to give you a future and a hope**. Then you will call upon Me and go and pray to Me, and I will listen to you. And you will seek Me and find Me, when you search for Me with all your heart. I will be found by you, says the LORD, and **I will bring you back from your captivity*** (Jeremiah 29:11–14, emphasis added). Often times it is easy to believe for someone else, but harder to believe that God will do it for me. This is a question of believing that God truly loves me and wants the best for me.

Let's examine some of the lessons on hope in Job:

- Job 4:6: *"Is not your reverence your confidence? And the integrity of your ways your hope?"* Job 31:24: *"If I have made gold my hope, Or said to fine gold, 'You are my confidence.'"* Our hope must be in God, not in our integrity or our possessions.
- Job 6:11 indicates that hope requires strength to press through: *"What strength do I have, that I should hope?"*
- Job 11:18: *"And you would be secure, because there is hope; Yes, you would dig around you, and take your rest in safety."* Hope provides a sense of security and rest in the soul.
- Job 14:19: *"As water wears away stones, And as torrents wash away the soil of the earth; So You destroy the hope of man."* Job 19:10: *"He breaks me down on every side,*

And I am gone; My hope He has uprooted like a tree."
Hope is destroyed by the constant wearing away of circumstances. Proverbs 13:12: *"Hope deferred makes the heart sick, But when the desire comes, it is a tree of life."*

- Job 17:15: *"Where then is my hope? As for my hope, who can see it?"* Hope believes in what is unseen.
- Job 41:9: *"Indeed, any hope of overcoming him [Leviathan] is false; Shall one not be overwhelmed at the sight of him?"* Some situations look too big for us, and we need to ask a very big God to deal with the impossible.

You are God!

Did Job respond correctly through the whole process? No! The idea of the wilderness or the refiner's fire is to bring the impurities to the surface so they can be removed. God was pleased because Job never stopped his relationship with God. He kept seeking God's face and asking why. However, Job did accuse God of not being fair. If we did go through the experience perfectly, we would either be Jesus or self-righteous.

After being in the wilderness or the Job experience for some years, I went through **another** crisis. I had gone through one of the strongest temptations I have ever experienced in my heart. I came through bruised, but did not give in. But afterwards, I questioned God as I never had before. I was suffering physically, emotionally, and spiritually. I started crying out, "Lord, I have followed Your ways to the best of my ability for thirty years. I have made righteous lifestyle choices. I have followed after You even through the dark night of my soul. I have had my heart sifted. So why haven't I seen any of Your promises to me manifested on the earth?" (This was exaggeration in the moment of extreme pain). "Why have people believed vicious lies about me? Why is my body not healed? Why has my husband not appeared on the scene? Why am I still in a wilderness? How come other people have not had to go through the same fire that You have required of me? Why? Why? Why?" My spirit was beginning to shut down.

Job knew about God in the beginning of the book, but he really knew (*yada*) God in the end after God speaks to him out of the whirlwind. He had hope that he would see God. Even in the midst of the trials, his heart cry was, "God, I want to see you!" *"For I know that my Redeemer lives, And He shall stand at last on the earth; And after my skin is destroyed, this I know, That in my flesh I shall see God, Whom I shall see for myself, And my eyes shall behold, and not another. How my heart yearns within me!"* (Job 19:25–27, emphasis added).

"But he is never free to open his spirit to God until God himself visits him in chapters 38–41. It's the revelation of God that ultimately opens Job's heart completely to God's sovereign purposes in his life. Job came through his crisis successfully by constantly lifting his face to God. While his friends talked about God, he talked to God."[47]

God did not answer Job's questions; instead, He revealed all His power, majesty, and beauty.

When Job encountered God, he was changed down to the core of his being. His DNA was changed. God did not answer Job's questions; instead, He revealed all His power, majesty, and beauty. God revealed Himself to Job by asking him questions (*midrash*) for two chapters. Then the following dialog in Job 40:1–11 occurred:

> *Moreover the LORD answered Job, and said:* ***"Shall the one who contends with the Almighty correct Him?*** *He who rebukes God, let him answer it."*
>
> *Then Job answered the LORD and said:* *"Behold, I am vile;* ***What shall I answer You? I lay my hand over my mouth.*** *Once I have spoken, but I will not answer; Yes, twice, but I will proceed no further."*
>
> *Then* ***the LORD answered Job out of the whirlwind,*** *and said: "Now prepare yourself like a man;* ***I will question you, and you shall answer Me:*** *Would you indeed annul My judgment? Would you condemn Me that you may be justified? Have you an arm like God? Or can you*

thunder with a voice like His? Then adorn yourself with majesty and splendor, And array yourself with glory and beauty. Disperse the rage of your wrath; Look on everyone who is proud, and humble him."

Job realized he spoke out of turn big time! Like Isaiah, he recognized God's greatness and his own weakness. God began by rebuking Job for angrily questioning God's justice (his fairness) in the situation. He did not question Job's integrity. Then God challenged Job for another two chapters! Job's final answer was in total humility. He admitted that he spoke without understanding God. When **he saw God**, he repented totally. Then restoration happened: *"Then Job answered the LORD and said: 'I know that You can do everything, And that no purpose of Yours can be withheld from You. You asked, "Who is this who hides counsel without knowledge?" Therefore I have uttered what I did not understand, Things too wonderful for me, which I did not know. Listen, please, and let me speak; You said, "I will question you, and you shall answer Me." I have heard of You by the hearing of the ear, but now my eye sees You. Therefore I abhor myself, and repent in dust and ashes'"* (Job 42:1–6, emphasis added).

A few months after my latest crisis, I went to a Friends of the Bridegroom conference. I repented for being angry at God. I sobbed my grief out. Trust and hope were re-ignited. Then slowly, I felt the breath of God blow over my life. My heart that seemed dead started to beat again.

Solomon

It is often said, "The greater the ministry or reward, the greater the testing process." God brings the testing process so we will not self-destruct under the reward through pride or idolatry.

The life of Solomon is a negative example of this. He did not have a wilderness experience, as his father David did. His heart was right in the beginning. He pleased God by asking for the right things:

On that night God appeared to Solomon, and said to him, "Ask! What shall I give you?" And Solomon said to God: "You have shown great mercy to David my father, and *have made me king in his place. Now, O LORD God, let Your promise to David my father be established, for You have made me king over a people like the dust of the earth in multitude. Now **give me wisdom and knowledge**, that I may go out and come in before this people; for who can judge this great people of Yours?" Then God said to Solomon: "**Because this was in your heart**, and you have not asked riches or wealth or honor or the life of your enemies, nor have you asked long life—but have **asked wisdom and knowledge for yourself, that you may judge My people over whom I have made you king**—wisdom and knowledge are granted to you; **and I will give you riches and wealth and honor**, such as none of the kings have had who were before you, nor shall any after you have the like."* (2 Chronicles 1:7–12, emphasis added)

However, Solomon ended up in idolatry after being given the greatest blessings of wisdom, finances, power, and a meeting with God. Although God appeared to Solomon, his DNA was not changed. Solomon reacted very differently from Job or Isaiah when God's manifest presence showed up. Solomon did not exhibit any fear of the Lord:

*But **King Solomon loved many foreign women**, as well as the daughter of Pharaoh: women of the Moabites, Ammonites, Edomites, Sidonians, and Hittites—from the nations of whom the LORD had said to the children of Israel, "**You shall not intermarry with them**, nor they with you. Surely **they will turn away your hearts after their gods." Solomon clung to these in love.** And he had seven hundred wives, princesses, and three hundred concubines; and his wives turned away his heart. For it was so, **when Solomon was old, that his wives turned his heart after other gods; and his heart was not loyal to the LORD his God**, as was the heart of his father David. For Solomon went after Ashtoreth the goddess of the Sidonians, and after Milcom the abomination of the Ammonites. **Solomon did evil in the sight of the LORD**,* *and **did not fully follow the LORD**, as did his father David. Then Solomon **built a high place** for Chemosh the abomination of Moab, on the hill that is east of Jerusalem, and for Molech the abomination of the people of Ammon. And he did likewise for all his foreign wives, who burned incense and sacrificed to their gods.* (1 Kings 11:1–8, emphasis added)

Throughout scripture, God talks about idolatry as spiritual adultery. Solomon fell away from loving the Lord his God with all his heart to following after the gods his wives worshipped. At first it was just his heart turning, but eventually he built places of worship for the abominable gods. The worship of Molech required putting children in the fire as sacrifices. Solomon fell because he forgot to acknowledge that "You are God!" and did not go through a wilderness testing.

Broken Before the Lord

Do you know that awful feeling when you hear a waitress drop a stack of dishes in a restaurant? Although we may cringe at the breaking in our lives, God rejoices. While I was living overseas, God showed me a visual example of what was going on in my life.

I watched as two hands picked up and dropped a clay vase. The first time it was dropped, it didn't break. The second time, it broke into three pieces. Then each of the pieces was systematically picked up and dropped until all that was left was dust.

I asked God why? After all, this was my life we were talking about!!!

He said the vase didn't break at first because my heart was too hard. The second time it broke, but not deeply enough. At this point, the vase could have been glued back together into its original shape. Then it would be only a cracked pot. (God has a sense of humor!) But if the vase were totally broken so that only fine dust remained, it could be remade into something brand new—porcelain.

The primary difference between clay and porcelain is the fineness of the material that has been prepared. Porcelain must be baked at a higher temperature than clay. The glaze on porcelain is usually shinier. Perhaps more importantly, you can see light through porcelain! All of these characteristics make porcelain more valuable than ordinary clay.

What does it mean to be broken before the Lord? When I was teaching, this was an acronym the Lord gave me:

B—know you are the **beloved** of the Lord.

R—go through the **refiner's fire** to be made into gold.

O—make your life an **offering**, a living sacrifice.

K—die to the old self, so that the **kernel of love** can grow.

E—**exalt** (praise) **the Lord** in all circumstances and make Him your hiding place.

N—be made into a **new creation.**

God wants each of us to be a new creation—a vessel of porcelain and honor. Sometimes we have to be broken and returned to dust so the potter can recreate us. After all, Adam was formed from dust or clay. *"Will the thing formed say to him who formed it, 'Why have you made me like this?' Does not the potter have power over the clay, from the same lump to make one vessel for honor and another for dishonor?"* (Romans 9:20–21).

Clay Pots

In the Bible, most of the scriptures demonstrate how the potter (God) takes great care in the creation of His precious pots (us). The emphasis is on the clay's submission to the process because he does not yet know what the potter will create from him:

> *The precious sons of Zion, Valuable as fine gold, How they are regarded as clay pots, The work of the hands of the potter!* (Lamentations 4:2)

> *Surely you have things turned around! Shall the potter be esteemed as the clay; For shall the thing made say of him who made it, "He did not make me"? Or shall the thing formed say of him who formed it, "He has no understanding"?* (Isaiah 29:16)

> *But now, O LORD, You are our Father;* **We are the clay, and You our potter; And all we are the work of Your hand.** *(Isaiah 64:8, emphasis added)*

> *The word which came to Jeremiah from the LORD,*

saying: "Arise and go down to the potter's house, and there I will cause you to hear My words." Then I went down to the potter's house, and there he was, making something at the wheel. And the vessel that he made of clay was marred in the hand of the potter; so he made it again into another vessel, as it seemed good to the potter to make. (Jeremiah 18:1–4)

But in a great house there are not only vessels of gold and silver, but also of wood and clay, some for honor and some for dishonor. Therefore if anyone cleanses himself from the latter, he will be a vessel for honor, sanctified and useful for the Master, prepared for every good work. (2 Timothy 2:20–21)

We need to trust that He knows the purpose for which He created us, even when we don't see the end.

We choose whether we want to be a vessel of honor or dishonor by how we submit to the potter. Notice it doesn't matter whether you are gold or clay—both can be used for honor or dishonor. We need to trust that He knows the purpose for which He created us, even when we don't see the end. It is agreeing with God, that though I may not like His plans for my life, He knows best.

Preparation

Like Jeremiah, let's go down to the potter's house and watch the clay being prepared, shaped, fired, and decorated for use.

The creation of pottery and porcelain is one of the oldest arts in the world. Pottery had a central role in Biblical times. Archeologists determine how old each layer of a dig is by the type and age of the pottery. Pottery is a general term often applied to all products of the potter's art.

- Earthenware is softer clay fired at a relatively low

temperature.

- Stoneware is a denser, harder pottery fired at a higher temperature.
- Porcelain is translucent. A strong light near the plate shines through it. It is fired at almost double the temperature of earthenware.

The process of preparation for a pot is much like the oil press!

1. **The potter must first find the proper clay, then purify and cure it to make it usable.** Raw clays or kaolins are washed in large vats to remove foreign matter. Pebbles, sand, and feldspar settle during the washing process. The usable clay, known as "slip," remains in suspension in the water and is poured off. If the clay is to be used in a plastic state (not completely dry), it is forced through pugmills, where rotating knives cut up and compress it. Then the clay is forced out and formed into cakes or other convenient shapes for storage and handling. The dried clay is ground up, sifted, then mixed with other ingredients in rotating mixing machines. Next, it is moistened to give it sufficient plasticity. If the clay is kaolin for the manufacture of porcelain, it is combined with feldspar, white-burning ball clay, and flint or quartz. If the product is bone china, bone ash is added.

2. **The next step is forming the ceramic object.** This may be done by throwing on a potter's wheel, by molding, or by casting. Throwing means shaping a mass of clay spinning on a potter's wheel, or circular revolving table. The clay is shaped by the moistened hands of the potter into a vase, bowl, plate, or jug. The potter's wheel is particularly needed for making round objects, though flat round objects such as plates usually are made in molds.

3. **After the object is shaped, it is ready for firing.** The intensity of firing depends on whether the object is pottery or porcelain and what kind of decoration it is to have. The higher the grade or the finer the decoration, the higher the tempera-

ture! Earthenware may be fired at a temperature of 1,400 degrees Fahrenheit; porcelain or stoneware may need 2,700 degrees Fahrenheit. The object is fired in a kiln. This may be an open-hearth fire for baking crude clay bowls, a wood-fired kiln of 18th–century France and England, or a modern electrically fired tunnel oven. The objects to be fired are placed in fire-clay boxes, arranged in tiers or piles. The boxes protect the ware from direct contact with the fire. Otherwise the objects are stacked in piles and separated by stilts of fire clay.

4. **There are numerous decorating processes.** The European soft-paste porcelain body was fired first at a fairly high temperature, then glazed and fired again at a lower temperature. Firing the body is called "bisque firing"; firing the glaze is called "glost firing." In underglaze decoration, the design is painted on the body before firing, if the piece is to be fired only once. Otherwise the design is painted on after the first firing and before the glazing and second firing. Overglaze decoration is painted on after the glaze has been fired. The decoration is then fixed to the glaze by another firing at a relatively low temperature.[48]

The more complex pots are carefully placed in the fire of the kiln several times. The temperature and timing are carefully monitored by the potter to ensure that each one comes out perfectly. The whole process is a prophetic picture of how God prepares us prior to being shown to the world as His bride.

Who is He? Who am I?

So who is this God who loves each of us passionately? How can I see Him for who He really is? If you really want to know who He is, ask the Holy Spirit to open the eyes and ears of your heart so you can see and hear in your prayer times and as you read the scriptures—as you wait upon Him.

Jesus is the bridegroom, king, and judge. The Song of Solomon is among the best descriptions of who this God is and what our relationship is with Him. Meditate on it. Psalm 45 is another description of the bridegroom God who is king and judge.

Will the Lord cast off forever? And will He be favorable no more? Has His mercy ceased forever? Has His promise failed forevermore? Has God forgotten to be gracious? Has He in anger shut up His tender mercies? Selah. And I said, "This is my anguish; But I will remember the years of the right hand of the Most High." **I will remember the works of the LORD; Surely I will remember Your wonders of old. I will also meditate on all Your work, And talk of Your deeds. Your way, O God, is in the sanctuary; Who is so great a God as our God? You are the God who does wonders; You have declared Your strength among the peoples. You have with Your arm redeemed Your people,** *The sons of Jacob and Joseph. Selah. The waters saw You, O God; The waters saw You, they were afraid; The depths also trembled. The clouds poured out water; The skies sent out a sound; Your arrows also flashed about. The voice of Your thunder was in the whirlwind. The lightnings lit up the world; The earth trembled and shook.* **Your way was in the sea, Your path in the great waters, And Your footsteps were not known. You led Your people** *like a flock By the hand of Moses and Aaron.* (Psalm 77:7–20, emphasis added)

We need to know how much larger God is than **any** crisis in our life or our world. "Preoccupation with ourselves and our inadequacies must give way to a revelation of God as the as the great 'I Am.' 'I Am' will go with us. 'I Am' will be present on the journey. 'I Am' will do the work as we stand before the people and situations that are bigger and more formidable. The conversion process is designed to lead us away from self reliance into a more intimate place of surrender to all that God is and can accomplish. When we are fully converted to God's ways, then we can be commissioned with His authority and power to take the land and enter a new beginning. Conversion means we no longer get in the way of all that God wants to do and accomplish. We cease to be conscious or unconscious resisters and instead become willing vessels in the hands of a sovereign God."[49] We need to remember and meditate on His wonders in our lives and in creation. I read Psalm 18 when I need to remember the greatness of God.

Once we begin to get a glimpse of this God who is infinitely larger than any crisis going on in our lives or any wars in the world, then we get a firm grasp on what is reality. I loved the movie "The Matrix" that came out in 1999. It was a graphic portrayal of how we think that what we can see and touch is reality. But after Neo takes the red pill, his senses go out of balance, and even his knowledge of who he is changes drastically. What he thought was reality was imaginary. Now he must relearn what reality truly is and how to operate in it. He must come to grips with a new mindset or framework. This is true in the Kingdom of God. We thought this world was reality. Yet God says the Kingdom of God is reality. It has a different set of rules and ways to operate in the supernatural realm. Just because Neo was unaware of the "other" world didn't mean it didn't exist. One line in the movie describes the Matrix as "the world pulled over your eyes to blind you." Wow! What a truth for those of us who are called to live in the Kingdom of God. At first Neo doesn't walk in this new mindset. But a crisis comes and he begins to operate in the reality of the new realm. He can perform acts that weren't possible in the old mindset. God wants each of us to know Him and know we are "the one", so we can walk in the reality of who we are in Him. This is a transformation process! We don't get transformed by taking a red pill or loading up with new information, but by spending time with the God of all the universe.

His Desire

I also need to know that this larger-than-life God longs for relationship with **me**. Imagine in your mind's eye two people who are in love. Picture how they desires to be with each other, and to reach out and touch each other, and how their love is reflected in their eyes. That is how God feels about you! Some of us get uncomfortable to think that God gets emotional thinking about us. I know I did when this was a new thought to me. Thinking about God wanting to give me kisses on my mouth seemed a bit over the top. Yet this is what the Song of Solomon 1:2 says He wants to do. We desperately need to know this God who desires us and believes we are that beautiful. Who we are right now is attractive to Him. *"So the King will greatly desire your beauty; Because He is your Lord,* *worship Him"* (Psalm 45:11). The Beloved (Jesus) says to the Shulamite woman (you), *"How fair and how pleasant you are, O love, with your delights!"* (Song of Solomon 7:6).

We desperately need to know this God who desires us and believes we are that beautiful.

Now the Beloved had said similar things to her previously. But it is only when the reality that the Beloved truly loves her, even in all her weaknesses, that the Shulamite woman is able to respond: *"I am my beloved's, And his desire is toward me. Come, my beloved, Let us go forth to the field; Let us lodge in the villages. Let us get up early to the vineyards; Let us see if the vine has budded, Whether the grape blossoms are open, And the pomegranates are in bloom. There I will give you my love"* (Song of Solomon 7:10–12). A peace comes to her to know that she belongs to Jesus and that He desires her. She wants to go forth with him (ministry) and to lodge or live permanently with Him. I think it is interesting that she also wants to see if the winter or wilderness season is really over. She goes with her Beloved to see if the dead-looking stump in the vineyard finally has some new buds and blossoms! It is in the place of the former wilderness that she is able to finally give Him her love, and then it becomes a garden full of fruit and fragrant flowers.

Even if you are not feeling beautiful to God, know that He sees you this way. He makes us beautiful from the inside out. The transformation always starts at the heart. Ecclesiastes 3:11–12 states, ***"He has made everything beautiful in its time. Also He has put eternity in their hearts,*** *except that no one can find out **the work that God does from beginning to end.*** *I know that nothing is better for them than to rejoice, and to do good in their lives"* (emphasis added). This area has taken a long time to take root in me. God has had to transform how I saw myself. I have been very hard and unmerciful in my view of myself. God is in the midst of transforming my mindset so I know that I am beautiful to God and that He desires me purely. As this happens, I can feel my heart begin to expand and come to a place of rest. This is where our DNA is changed in an encounter with God. As we begin to see ourselves as God sees us, that vision becomes reality in us.

It is extremely important to know who we are, because what we do flows out of who we are, including our relationships. "Getting a grip on who He is and who we are in Him will also revolutionize how we relate to one another. It literally changes our emotional chemistry to encounter the majesty, beauty, sweet affection, stunning mystery and splendor of our beloved God, Jesus Christ."[50] It is also what will make our ministries more loving rather than legalistic. We are becoming a greater reflection of who He is.

Embracing the Cross

So how do we begin to feel beautiful before the Lord? It happens as we allow God to crucify the old self. *"That I may know Him and the power of His resurrection, and the fellowship of His sufferings, being conformed to His death"* (Philippians 3:10, emphasis added). First the heart cry to know (*yada*) Him must come, and then the willingness to pay the high price. This requires us to identify with Him in His death before we can be raised to new life (resurrection).

Wade Taylor in *The Secret of the Stairs* reveals the purpose of the stairs in our life:

> My beloved spoke, and said to me: "Rise up, my love, my fair one, and come away" (Song of Solomon 2:10).
>
> As I responded to this expression of His desire toward me, and begin to climb the stairs, I must consider that a "stair" has first a riser and then a step, or platform. My ascent toward the Lord must progress one step at a time, ever upward toward Him, riser and step upon riser and step. The Lord awaits within His chambers, at the top of these stairs.
>
> The first riser and step may be called "revelation." When a scripture is quickened within me, my understanding is "opened" concerning it. As I embrace this understanding (the riser) and act upon it (the step), it will become a personal reality within my life experience....
>
> The "revelation" that I received (riser) had to become a

part of me and reflect Jesus through my daily pattern of life (step).

As I arrived at the top of the riser to enter this "stage" of life experience, the step crossed the riser and appeared to me as being a cross. It rested on top of the revelation that had brought me upward this far and was situated so I could not enter the step that was beyond until I first embraced this cross. As I died further to my own ways, I was released to move into the circumstances the Lord had prearranged for me on this level. As these had the full affect on me, the revelations I had received became within me a present reality, and "substance" was added to my spiritual experience.[51]

Each stair is a test. My self-will is revealed, I embrace the cross, die to myself, and experience more of the life of God within me. This stairway to heaven is different for each person. We are being asked to **willingly** obey what God is asking for in a situation. In Luke 9:23, Jesus said, *"If anyone desires to come after Me, let him deny himself, and take up his cross daily, and follow Me"* (emphasis added). The operative words are "if" and "take up his cross daily." We each have a choice to take up or ignore the cross before us. It is **our** cross, not our neighbor's. It is interesting, but the cross someone else has to carry often looks lighter and less horrible than our own. For example, God took me through a long year or so of unemployment to kill some of my self-life. For Wade Taylor, it was taking an extra job when he didn't need the money. The key is obedience to what God is asking **you** to do. It is the place where you say, "Not my will, but yours be done." With each act of obedience comes a greater revelation of His ways.

True Trust

The work God is trying to perform in our spirits is "Do you trust me?" Did you ever play the trust game? Everyone stands in a circle, and the person in the middle is to fall back and "trust" that the other people will catch him. I have to admit this was always a hard game for me to play. So God has had to work on my ability to trust. I am delighted to say that He is better at catching us when we fall than our peers are! As I walked through the season of unemployment followed by difficult circumstances in jobs, I asked the questions of "Why?" and "How come this is happening if I am walking in Your ways?" Each time I received the same "answer": "Will you trust Me?" Sometimes I just wanted to scream! "Excuse me, God, but do You realize the pain I am in?" "Yes, daughter, I love you. But will you trust Me?"

> It is arduous to live without an answer to this "Why?" that we are easily seduced into connecting the events over which we have no control with our conscious and unconscious evaluation. When we have cursed ourselves or allowed others to curse us, it is very tempting to explain all the brokenness we experience as an expression of confirmation of this curse.
> The powers of darkness around us are strong, and our world finds it easier to manipulate self-rejecting people than self-accepting people. But when we keep listening attentively to the voice calling us the Beloved, it becomes possible to live our brokenness, not as a confirmation of our fear that we are worthless, but as an opportunity to purify and deepen the blessings that rests upon us.... What seemed intolerable becomes a challenge. What seemed a reason for depression becomes a source of purification. What seemed punishment becomes a gentle pruning? What seemed rejection becomes a way to a deeper communion.[52]

God wants us to get to the point where we will trust Him, no matter what the circumstances are in our lives! This means going up quite a few stairs! Our natural inclination (not to mention our culture) teaches us to trust only ourselves. We must fall into the arms of the one who loves us, just as we would fall in the Trust Game. One of the visuals God gives me for this walk of faith and trust is where Indiana Jones must step off into seeming nothingness, only to find a bridge exists for him walk on. God wants us to walk out in faith so we can see His faithfulness. We must be totally dependent on Him for everything.

God often puts blinders on the eyes of prophetic people so that they can see clearly for other people, but can not see for themselves. I believe this is so that we will live in relationship to one another. When we are in this position the main thing we need to keep focused on is the back of Jesus as we follow Him. It is when we try to look around Him that we come out of alignment and begin to stumble. It is in that place of being content with today, yet stretching "to see in the spirit" where tremendous growth happens.

I needed some money for rent, so I was waiting on the Lord. The scripture the Lord kept giving me was in 2 Chronicles 20: *"Thus says the LORD to you: 'Do not be afraid nor dismayed because of this great multitude, for the battle is not yours, but God's. You will not need to fight in this battle. Position yourselves, stand still and see the salvation of the LORD, who is with you, O Judah and Jerusalem!' Do not fear or be dismayed; tomorrow go out against them, for the LORD is with you"* (20:15,17, emphasis added). What can you do when God says the battle is His? You are to stand still and watch for the salvation of the Lord. Oh, and by the way, don't be afraid or dismayed! King Jehoshaphat bowed his head with his face to the ground before the Lord and worshipped Him. Could I do anything less? Then Jehoshaphat stood and said, *"'Hear me, O Judah and you inhabitants of Jerusalem: Believe in the LORD your God, and you shall be established; believe His prophets, and you shall prosper.' And when he had consulted with the people, he appointed those who should sing to the LORD, and who should praise the beauty of holiness, as they went out before the army and were saying: 'Praise the LORD, for His mercy endures forever.'"* (20:20–21, emphasis added). The people worshiped the beauty of the Lord, and the Lord set ambushes against Israel's enemies so they were defeated. It took three days for the people to gather the spoils.

I found that God was placing me between a rock and a hard place. My total circumstances were such that there was nowhere to turn, except to Him. He gave me the instruction to rest in Him, not blaming Him or others, not fasting, not doing warfare, and not trying to change the circumstances in my own strength. I was to offer a sacrifice of praise. He wanted my heart to see His faithfulness even when I didn't "perform." I needed to look to Him for my ability to trust and to stop being totally dependent on myself. My spoil was to receive an unexpectedly large gift at the end of this trial! My experience was to trust God more deeply and rise up one more step on the stairs to heaven.

Sometimes God asks us to sacrifice the promise He gave to us. Often this is when we start placing the promise before God. Sigh! *"Now it came to pass after these things that God tested Abraham, and said to him, 'Abraham!' And he said, 'Here I am.' And He said, 'Take now your son, your only son Isaac, whom you love, and go to the land of Moriah, and offer him there as a burnt offering on one of the mountains of which I shall tell you'"* (Genesis 22:1–2). God knew that Isaac was the beloved son of promise to Abraham. He knew what it meant to ask him to sacrifice Isaac. Yet Abraham went to the mountain, built the altar, and raised the knife to sacrifice Isaac. Scripture gives no indication that he hesitated or second-guessed himself. He did what God asked, without question. Wow! God saw his heart and responded. *"And He said, 'Do not lay your hand on the lad, or do anything to him; **for now I know that you fear God, since you have not withheld your son**, your only son, from Me.'"* (Genesis 22:12, emphasis added). God has sometimes asked me to lay on the altar His promises to me. It is hard! Sometimes He has burned the hope of the promise fulfilled on the altar only to return the promise in a better form. Sometimes it has just been burned up. His ways are not our ways. He is jealous over our hearts, desiring that nothing comes between Him and us, not even good things from Him.

Learning to Rise on Eagle's Wings

So how do I make the first commandment first? How do I get the idols out of my life? It is a process of letting go and becoming unencumbered—free. *"Now the Lord is the Spirit; and **where the Spirit of the Lord is, there is liberty**. But we all, with unveiled face, beholding as in a mirror the glory of the Lord, **are being transformed into the same image from glory to glory**, just as by the Spirit of the Lord"* (2 Corinthians 3:17–18, emphasis added). As we are transformed, we go from one realm of glory to greater realms of glory. God invites us to be transformed so we can rise up the stairs or on eagle's wings to the high places. His invitation is

COME UP! Reuben Morgan wrote a song called "Eagle's Wings." He describes how we will arise on eagle's wings after we have learned to wait for Him and abide in Him.

God invites us to be transformed so we can rise up the stairs or on eagle's wings to the high places. His invitation is COME UP!

"He found him in a desert land And in the wasteland, a howling wilderness; He encircled him, He instructed him, He kept him as the apple of His eye. As an eagle stirs up its nest, Hovers over its young, Spreading out its wings, taking them up, Carrying them on its wings, So the LORD alone led him, And there was no foreign god with him. He made him ride in the heights of the earth, That he might eat the produce of the fields; He made him to draw honey from the rock, And oil from the flinty rock" (Deuteronomy 32:10–13).

God sometimes leads us into and then finds us in the wilderness. He encircles us in pursuit and then hovers over us, spreading His wings of protection. Then He carries us **on His wings** to teach us His ways until the idolatry is gone. Finally, He has us fly on our own wings to eat the fruitfulness of the land. In the hard place, He provides the ability to feed on the sweetness of the word (honey from the rock) and to dwell in the anointing of Jesus (oil from the flinty rock). This removes the fear, shame, and legalism. Going back to Isaiah 40:28–31, it is when we wait on Him that our strength will be renewed so that we can rise on eagle's wings. Our strength returns when we have hopeful and unencumbered hearts—when we are abandoned to Him.

It was the eagle which drew the attention of our guide. We were near the summit of the 7,600–foot mountain, and the eagle was already at 10,000 feet above us and climbing.

"How high will he go?" I asked.

"Over the storm. Twenty-five, thirty thousand feet. He

is now beyond his own control. He locks his wings, here," he said—pointing at his shoulders—"and rides the wind of God."

Again he used that magnificent Hebrew word ruach to describe the thermals of the desert. It was the same word King David used in Psalm 51 to describe the Holy Spirit—the breath of God. "Take not thy ruach from me."

In the New Testament the word is softer, more gentle. There we find the Greek work pneuma, meaning breath or spirit. It is the same word from which we get "pneumatic." In the New Testament it is often used to describe the filling experience. So the Holy Spirit fills, much as one would blow up a balloon. The thought is one of lifting—from within. But in the Old Testament, the Spirit of God, the ruach, is anything but gentle. Here it is a roaring wind, howling through the canyons and moaning over the mountains. It is the mighty winds of the storms blowing across the wilderness accompanied by flashing lightning and rumbling thunder. It is the hot air thermals rushing upward. And upon it rides the eagle, ascending to unbelievable heights, using the air currents which destroy things on the ground to carry him over the fury of the storm to safety on the other side.

I watched fascinated, as the eagle circled and ascended until he was but a tiny dot against the onrushing storm. Then he disappeared all together.

"He fears nothing," the guide said.[53]

Is it time for you to rise on eagle's wings on the thermals of God's breath? Are you willing to trust Him in your brokenness and weakness to love you and bring you into your destiny?

Porcelain Treasure

God recently gave me a new porcelain container. It is white and shaped like a round gift box with a big red bow. Embossed hearts overlay it. It is sealed with gold. Inside is a beautiful heart of gold and diamonds. He said this was a prophetic expression of my new porcelain container that replaces the clay vase that was smashed to dust. It contains an intercessor's heart. Diamonds often represent intercession in God's economy. The three-dimensional hearts on the box symbolize His love and desire for me and His pleasure in my love. He has wrapped my heart in a white or pure box with a red ribbon representing His blood. It is a gift of love for His son and for His son's bride. I keep it on my nightstand as a remembrance of what He has done. Needless to say, it is far more beautiful than the clay pot that distressed me when I saw it break!

Getting Off the Merry-Go-Round

(Disciplines of the Forerunner)

Igniting passion or going deep in God is something we each must do for ourselves. Neither a pastor, teacher, mentor, friend, nor even a spouse can ignite the fire. We must warm our hearts by following the disciplines of a forerunner. It takes time. The colder the heart, the longer it takes to become a raging fire. Ask God for more hunger, for it is a gift from Him. Our partnership is to follow His plan. Most Christian contemplatives exhort us that this is a lifestyle choice, and we must see this as a long-term commitment even if we don't see the fruit right away. It won't happen overnight, unless God does it sovereignly. The spiritual disciplines, such as fasting and meditation, can speed the process up. The disciplines help us from going in circles on the merry-go-round so we can reach our destiny in God. At the beginning of the year, I heard the Lord speak that this was the year for disciplines. This is not because "I have been bad" but it is a call to some lifestyle changes. I have struggled to be consistent in the spiritual disciplines. I have been better with some disciplines in certain seasons, and others in different seasons. I confess part of the reason is lack of discipline or just plain forgetting in my busyness. But bless God—He brings me back to them! I believe my abiding in His love will now provide the strength and grace, rather than trying to do it by sheer willpower.

> Igniting passion or going deep in God is
> something we each must do for ourselves.

We must not be led to believe that the Disciplines are for spiritual giants and hence beyond our reach, or for contemplatives who devote all their time to prayer and meditation. Far from it. God intends the Disciplines of the spiritual life to be for ordinary human beings: people who have jobs, who care for children, who must wash dishes and mow lawns. In fact, the disciplines are best exercised in the midst of our normal daily activities. If they are to have any transforming effect, the effect must be found in the ordinary junctures of human life: in our relationships with our husband or wife, our brothers and sisters, our friends and neighbors.

Neither should we think of the Spiritual Disciplines as some dull drudgery aimed at exterminating laughter from the face of the earth. Joy is the keynote of all the Disciplines. The purpose of the Disciplines is liberation from the stifling slavery to self-interest and fear. When one's inner spirit is set free from all that holds it down that can hardly be described as dull drudgery. Singing, dancing, even shouting characterize the Disciplines of the spiritual life.

Psalm 42:7 reads "Deep calls unto deep." Perhaps somewhere in the subterranean chambers of your life you have heard the call to deeper, fuller living. Perhaps you have become weary of frothy experiences and shallow teaching. Every now and then you have caught glimpses, hints of something more than you have known. Inwardly you have launched out into the deep.[54]

The classic disciplines Richard Foster is describing are discussed in his book *Celebration of Discipline*. They are: Meditation, Prayer, Fasting, Study, Simplicity, Solitude, Submission, Service, Confession, Worship, Guidance, and Celebration. I have chosen to discuss only some of the disciples he writes about here. Let me admit up front that I don't practice them flawlessly nor have a complete understanding. But I do know that as I practice them, I draw closer to God and feel His heart more. It is to be part of our response when God calls us to the deep places in Him.

Worship

What is worship? *"Oh, **magnify the LORD** with me, And let us exalt **His name together. I sought the LORD**, and **He heard me,** And **delivered me from all my fears.** They looked to Him and **were radiant, And their faces were not ashamed"** (Psalm 34:3–5, emphasis added). "Worship is the act of exalting God. Enlarging our vision of him. Stepping into the cockpit to see where he sits and observe how he works. Of course, his size doesn't change, but our perception of him does. As we draw nearer, he seems larger. Isn't that what we need? A big view of God? Don't we have big problems, big worries, and big questions? Of course we do. Hence we need a big view of God."[55]

It is an awesome revelation when we realize that our puny little acts of worship, when we express our love to Him, touches His heart in ways we can't even begin to understand. One year, our prayer group created handmade valentines to give to God as an act of worship. I could feel the pleasure of God as we presented our feeble attempts to Him. His response blessed me deeply.

God calls us to have dove's eyes. The Song of Solomon mentions dove's eyes three times (1:15, 4:1, and 5:12). A dove mates for life and has no peripheral vision. She has eyes only for the one she loves. As we worship, God wants us to see only Him. As we let the other distractions fall away, we are better able to worship Him in spirit and in truth.

The purpose of worship is to change the worshipper. Jesus' whole appearance was transformed on the mountain of transfiguration. *"His face shone like the sun, and His clothes became as white as the light"* (Matthew 17:2). Moses' face shone so much he had to cover it up. Our shining countenance affects the people around us, especially during hard times.

Now it was so, when Moses came down from Mount Sinai

*(and the two tablets of the Testimony were in Moses'
hand when he came down from the mountain), that **Moses
did not know that the skin of his face shone while he
talked with Him**. So when Aaron and all the children of
Israel saw Moses, behold, **the skin of his face shone**, and
they were afraid to come near him. Then Moses called to
them, and Aaron and all the rulers of the congregation
returned to him; and Moses talked with them. Afterward
all the children of Israel came near, and he gave them as
commandments all that the LORD had spoken with him
on Mount Sinai. And when Moses had finished speaking
with them, he put a veil on his face. But whenever **Moses
went in before the LORD to speak with Him, he would
take the veil off until he came out**; and he would come
out and speak to the children of Israel whatever he had
been commanded. And whenever the children of Israel
saw the face of Moses, that the **skin of Moses' face
shone**, then Moses would put the veil on his face again,
until he went in to speak with Him.* (Exodus 34:29–35,
emphasis added)

"The connection between the face and worship is more than coin-
cidental. Our face is the most public part of our bodies, covered less
than any other area. It is also the most recognizable part of our
bodies. We don't fill a school annual with photos of people's feet
but rather with photos of faces. God desires to take our faces, this
exposed memorable part of our bodies, and use them to reflect his
goodness (2 Corinthians 3:18). God invites us to see His face so
He can change ours. He uses our uncovered faces to display His
glory. The transformation isn't easy."[56] A vibrant, shining face is
the mark of one who has stood in God's presence.

David was a worshipper. He coveted God's manifest presence
with him and the nation of Israel. He longed to see the Ark of the
Covenant returned to Jerusalem so God's presence would be in the
midst of His people. The Tabernacle of David is different from the
Tabernacle of Moses, which set boundaries to separate people from
God's presence. David's desire was to see intimacy restored to the
people of Israel. He taught them to corporately worship with

honesty, praise, thanksgiving, and rejoicing. He established sixteen ministries to be established twenty-four hours a day, seven days a week in the House of God. "None of these ministries were related to guilt or condemnation; all reflected recognition of the mercy and loving kindness of God and His unconditional acceptance of all who approached Him in faith."[57] Worship breaks the power of shame.

Passion

God and I were on a date when I had an open eye vision of the throne room in heaven. It is filled with emotion, passion, and expectation of what God will do, and not religious activities. The elders are not solemnly and properly laying down their crowns as I had envisioned before. They are whooping and hollering and are so excited about Jesus that they leap up and shout, enthusiastically throwing their crowns at Jesus' feet, and then fall on their faces in expectant worship before the Lord. The thunder and lightning are to produce a sense of expectation, not just reverence. The fire and glory of God is almost pulsating with the heartbeat of God, so everyone in heaven could be in tune with it.

Then I heard the following call to the body of Christ: "I want My throne room to be filled with passion, not religious rites. I want My people to be filled with expectation, wonder, and adoration as they enter My throne room. I want My people to be filled with joy as they come before Me. I am so tired of these solemn prayers. Come to Me with who you are, all of you, not just your church selves. I want all of your hearts, not just your church hearts. I want you to invite Me into every area of your lives. For YOU must invite Me in to your jobs, your homes, your fun, and your friendships—not just your ministries. Then I want you to ask Me for My heart in each of these areas, and I will give it."

I felt that there was a difference between intimacy and passion. Intimacy to me is quiet companionship and knowing each other down deep. Passion is being on fire (purely) for God or for another person. It is full of emotion and excitement.

God has seasons where He romances me. He will take me on "dates." One of the favorite places He takes me to is an eclectic coffeehouse where we spend quality time getting to know each other in public. We need to get out of the religious idea, that we spend time with God just in our prayer closet or in church. He wants to be a part of our everyday life and be taken to the highways and byways. We must not be afraid to express our passion for God in public places (without getting weird). It is wonderful to be passionately loved!

Reading the Bible

"Let him kiss me with the kisses of his mouth—For your love is better than wine" (Song of Solomon 1:2). The kisses of God's mouth come at those times when we are reading the Bible and His presence comes and we get new revelation that touches our hearts. This type of reading of the Bible is not doing word studies or research for a teaching. It is spending time with the Word, asking God for a revelation of Himself. For years I studied the Bible diligently and only occasionally received nuggets of gold that touched my heart and changed my life. I often had my intellectual hat on and studied to show myself approved. To be honest, it was dry and hard work. I was working through my mind instead of through my spirit. It was not until I started to read the Bible to seek a revelation of a person, rather than a doctrine, that the Bible started coming alive for me. All those years of study came in handy, too! What I had learned could now be applied in the spirit. As you have probably already realized, I love word studies! God has hidden so much in the names of people and places in the Bible. It is like a treasure hunt that makes the stories come so much more alive. We need to dig for the deep things of God. God reveals the deep things of His heart according to our spiritual hunger. Spiritual hunger has a force and intensity to it. No one can stop you from going for it.

Your name has meaning to God. My parents did not name me after Deborah in the book of Judges, yet that is my name and calling. As a child I did not like my name at all. In Hebrew, the interpretation means "industrious bee." There is a lot to understand about the bee that is apropos for me. But the root words of Deborah are *"debar,"* which means "word," and *"Yah,"* which is a name for God. Deborah, the Judge, was a Prophetess, so the fact that her name means "Word of God" makes sense. But it was not until God breathed life into that meaning that I understood my name and calling. Most of my life I had been "Debbie," but as God began to draw me deeper into Him, He reinstated my name as "Deborah." At first, I heard Him call me "Deborah," and also people who prophesied over me. Then He started telling some of my friends to call me Deborah. I finally said, "Oh, I get it! I am supposed to use that name!" I love my name now! This was a kiss from Him.

It may require discipline and practice to take time in the Word to let Him speak to you, especially if you have studied the Bible for many years. That study will pay off. But let Him begin to speak to you about how He feels about you. I believe you will be pleasantly surprised! Focus on His emotions toward you and creation. I would recommend starting in the Psalms or one of the Prophets such as Isaiah. Many of us have studied only the New Testament. God has much to say to us in the *Tanakh* or Old Testament. Psalm 119 is great to understand the purpose of the Word. Read the emotions of the Psalmist. The Word is not just so we know the "right things to do" but so we know (*yada*) the God of the Word. *"Your word is a lamp to my feet And a light to my path"* (Psalm 119:105). The Word brings light to the way we should go, but it is also about relationship. The lamp is not like headlights, helping us to see a long distance ahead. It is a lamp held by the hand of the one who loves us. He shows only enough of the path so we know where to go next and so we do not stumble. But we need to stay close to Him so we do not get beyond the protection of what the light has shown us. It is about trust and relationship—having a leaning heart.

Prayer

I have often said that prayer is my lifeblood. It is what keeps me going. Christians through the ages have dissected prayer in many different categories. But the overarching categories are:

- Supplication (praying for one's needs).
- Intercession (praying on behalf of another person or nation).
- Contemplative (spending time in God's presence to gain His heart).

Why do we pray? Do we believe it has an effect in heaven and on the earth? Dutch Sheets in *Intercessory Prayer* states, "Here we have, I believe, the reason for the necessity of prayer. God chose, from the time of creation, to work on the earth through humans, not independent of them. He always has and always will, even at the cost of becoming one. Though God is sovereign and all-powerful, Scripture clearly tells us that He limited Himself, concerning the affairs of the earth, to working through human beings."[58] *"The effective, fervent prayer of a righteous man avails much"* (James 5:16). God cares if we intercede.

The key to effective prayer is hearing the heartbeat of God and knowing His voice. Everything else flows from it.

The key to effective prayer is hearing the heartbeat of God and knowing His voice. Everything else flows from it. When we tap into what is on His heart and pray it back to Him, a heavenly circle is created, which touches heaven so His will can be done on the earth. We partner with Him to bring about His purposes for ourselves and others.

I was part of an intercessory team that prayed daily for three hours. We prayed for our mission, the city, our nation, and other nations. It was wonderful to see His heart released in the place of prayer and to see things change in the natural realm. It also changed me.

In college, a friend gave me a small book that captures the conversations of Brother Lawrence, a monk in the seventeenth century. He practiced the presence of God in such a way that his times of prayer were no different from his times of working. "Let all our employment be to know God; the more one knows Him, the more one desires to know Him. And as knowledge is commonly the measure of love, the deeper and more extensive our knowledge shall be, the greater will be our love; and if our love of God is great, we should love Him equally in pains and pleasures. Let us seek Him often by faith. He is within us; seek Him not elsewhere. Let us cast everything besides out of our hearts. He would possess them alone."[59]

Prayer is what brings us into the deepest work of the spirit. "To pray is to change. Prayer is the central avenue God uses to transform us. If we are unwilling to change, we will abandon prayer as a characteristic of our lives. The closer we come to the heartbeat of God, the more we see our need and the more we desire to be conformed to Christ. ... In prayer, real prayer, we begin to think God's thoughts after Him: to desire the things He desires, to love the things He loves. Progressively we are taught to see things from His point of view."[60]

Fasting

> "*But He knows the way that I take; When He has tested me, I shall come forth as gold. My foot has held fast to His steps; I have kept His way and not turned aside. I have not departed from the commandment of His lips; I have treasured the words of His mouth More than my necessary food*" (Job 23:10–12, emphasis added).

Mike Bickle calls fasting "voluntary weakness." It is allowing ourselves to be vulnerable by giving up a "pleasure" that we deem necessary for life. I have struggled with my weight for years. I don't believe I overeat compared to many people. My metabolism is slow. Yet, I know I have a weakness for sugar, especially chocolate, when I am stressed out. "Sin is a false comfort that people use as a prop to get them through seasons of pain. Many people get into sin because they feel abandoned by God and men. Even though they are not abandoned, they feel that way. So they reach out for immediate comfort in status, financial gain, or wrong expressions of sexuality. Although they are not sinless, spiritually satisfied people do sin less."[61] Ouch! So if I am eating chocolate (not sinful in itself) because I feel pain, then I am not totally satisfied in God. Hmmm...

The primary purpose of fasting is to express our hunger for God to come into our lives even more than He has. The secondary benefits—such as moving God's heart in prayer, spiritual insights, or even physical benefits—should never be the primary motive. "More than any other single Discipline, fasting reveals the things that control us. This is a wonderful benefit to the true disciple who longs to be transformed into the image of Jesus Christ. We cover up what is inside of us with food and other good things, but in fasting these things surface."[62] I am amazed at how easily I am affected by circumstances when I am fasting. Sometimes it is anger or fear, and sometimes pride. They surface because God wants to remove the impurities so I can be purer silver or gold. "Areas in which we are compromising will begin to decrease because fasting releases grace that insulates us from discontentment, complaining, and griping that is so prevalent throughout the world. Fasting literally begins to unlock and release those negative feelings that have been ruling our hearts and ruling us. This powerful spiritual tool strengthens our spiritual identity in God and weakens our fleshly identity. The presence of God also helps to break the bondage of self-absorption so common in today's world."[63]

At the beginning of the year, I heard the call to fast more. There are various kinds of fasts. Some involve controlled eating, such as a Daniel Fast (Daniel 1:8–16); in others, only water is consumed. I am not going to discuss the various types since many good books have been written on fasting. Nor am I going to go through some of the scriptures on fasting such as Isaiah 58, Matthew 9:14–15, or Luke 5:33–35. This is a study you should do on your own so God can speak to you. But I will highlight Matthew 6:16–18, where Jesus is speaking to His disciples: *"Moreover, **when you fast**, do not be like the hypocrites, with a sad countenance. For they disfigure their faces that they may appear to men to be fasting. Assuredly, I say to you, they have their reward. But you, **when you fast**, anoint your head and wash your face, **so that you do not appear to men to be fasting**, but to your Father who is in the secret place; and your Father who sees in secret will reward you openly"* (emphasis added). Jesus expected us to fast and to fast in private. He will show each of us how to fast.

John Piper's book, *A Hunger for God*, speaks to the motivation of why we fast. Are we fasting for ourselves or for God? The Bridegroom fast is a physical expression of a heart-hunger for Jesus in this life and for His return to the earth. "The absence of fasting is the measure of our contentment with the absence of Christ."[64] How satisfied or hungry are you? If you are dissatisfied with your life or God, fasting will increase your hunger for God.

When I fast and I want to give in, I declare to God, the powers of darkness, and myself: "God, I am more hungry for you than for this food. Fill me with who You are." "Fasting is a periodic—and sometimes decisive—declaration that we would rather feast at God's table in the kingdom of heaven than feed on the finest delicacies of this world. Joy in God is the strength to walk with Jesus from the wilderness to the cross and into eternal life. But maintaining that joy against its most subtle and innocent rivals is a lifelong struggle. And in that struggle, fasting—the humble, hungry handmaid of faith—is an emissary of grace."[65] God's presence is the only place my hungry soul (or yours) can find satisfaction.

Mike Bickle is calling for a corporate Bridegroom Fast three days each month. The dates can be found on the Friends of the Bridegroom website (FOTB.com). Generally, it is the first full Monday, Tuesday, and Wednesday of the month. This is a tremendous corporate opportunity to express our hunger to see Jesus glorified in our individual lives and on the earth. It also helps to know we are not fasting in isolation.

Repentance

Repentance is one of the keys to allowing God to remove the impurities (sins) in our hearts. Often it is part of the fasting process! As we allow Him to remove the idols, the places where we do not allow Him to reign in our lives, we receive more satisfaction in God. *"Repent, for the kingdom of heaven is at hand!"* is the cry of John the Baptist and Jesus (Matthew 3:2 and 4:17). The Hebrew word for "repent" (*shuwb*) means to turn back. The Greek word (*metanoeo*) means to think differently or reconsider.[66] So repentance is to change our minds about something we have done. It is to return to God's view on the subject. Often it takes a heart revelation from God to repent. "'Repent' did not mean to return to more dedicated efforts to please God by keeping the law or performing better works. The plea has always been simply to turn to God himself—to allow him to cleanse and restore."[67] Repentance must not be our own work of the will. That is self-righteousness, which is a stench in God's nostrils. Rather, it must be an opening of our hearts to allow Him to change our heart attitudes so that our behaviors can change. I can attest this is not an easy process. It is a willing submission of my will to His will, and acknowledging where my heart does not line up with His will.

But as we saw in the "Fasting" section, sin is usually caused by dissatisfaction in God. He loves us whether or not we sin. But if we turn to God's mercy in humility, as David did in Psalm 51, He will restore us. *"The sacrifices of God are a broken spirit, A broken and a contrite heart—These, O God, You will not despise"* (Psalm 51:17). God looks at our hearts when we sin and repent. He does not want us locked into recognizing all the bad and ugly things in our lives so we can make a self-effort to change. He wants us focused on Him so He can transform us. The difference is our heart attitude.

*"Repent therefore and be converted, that **your sins may be blotted out**, so that **times of refreshing** may come from the **presence of the Lord**, and that He may **send Jesus Christ**, who was preached to you before, whom heaven must receive until **the times of restoration of all things**, which God has spoken by the mouth of all His holy prophets since the world began"* (Acts 3:19–21, emphasis added). This passage speaks about some of the benefits of repenting. Repentance brings a refreshing in the Lord's presence, whether individually or corporately. Repentance is the key to turn judgment into restoration. "Repent or turn back" was the cry of God to the nation of Israel so He could call her His people once again. Walking in repentance must be a lifestyle choice to keep our hearts tender toward God, so we can hear the still, small voice to turn to Him to change us.

Forgiveness

Another discipline that will happen as you fast is a choice to live in forgiveness. God requires us to release people who have hurt us in every way possible, by forgiving them.

How often do we forgive them? Jesus did not agree with Peter's magnanimous offer to forgive seven times in Matthew 18:22. He said we must forgive seventy times seven, or more times than we can conceive. And then He told the story of the unforgiving servant. Perhaps you remember it in Matthew 18:21–35. The master forgives the servant a huge debt of millions of dollars, but the servant was unwilling to forgive the debt of a few dollars of a fellow servant: *"Then his master, after he had called him, said to him, 'You wicked servant! I forgave you all that debt because you begged me. Should you not also have had compassion on your fellow servant, just as I had pity on you?' And his master was angry, and delivered him to the torturers until he should pay all that was due to him. So My heavenly Father also will do to you if each of you, from his heart, does not forgive his brother his trespasses"* (Matthew 18:32–35).

As human beings, it is far too easy to carry grudges in our hearts against the little and big wrongs we feel have been committed against us. But it grieves God's heart! It is His nature to forgive, which is why He sacrificed His son so that we might live in relationship—as a son or daughter of the Father, as a bride of the Son, and as a friend of the Holy Spirit.

We separate ourselves from those relationships when we hold on to unforgiveness and end up living in torture. We hurt ourselves more than those we will not forgive. Often they are totally oblivious to our hurt, yet it is a death producing poison in our hearts. As God moves you to forgive, open your heart to allow Him to help you. When you can't let go, admit it to Him. Ask Him to help you forgive. Sometimes it will require a weekly, hourly, or moment-by-moment choice. Forgiving myself has sometimes been harder than forgiving someone else. Often this is because in pride I was blind to see it in myself.

Pause now. Ask God if there is anyone, including yourself, that you need to choose to forgive? Is there someone you need to ask forgiveness of? Respond to God as He suggests.

Dreams of God—Serving

Choosing joy! Remember that vision of the throne room? The elders were serving God joyfully, not soberly! God wants to give us the desires of our hearts! He put those desires in our hearts, then purifies them with His holy fire. So what are the longings of your heart? These are clues to how God wants you to be serving. God's plan for your life will be found where you experience pleasure and where you experience His pleasure in you. So what do you enjoy doing most in the world? When are you filled with joy? What do you feel satisfaction in accomplishing? It doesn't matter if another person considers it "important"—it is where you and God partner together. Follow your heart. God has designed each of us uniquely. *"For **we are His workmanship, created in Christ Jesus for good works, which God prepared beforehand** that we should walk in them"* (Ephesians 2:10, emphasis added). *"For You formed my inward parts; You covered me in my mother's womb. I will praise You, for **I am fearfully and wonderfully made;** Marvelous are Your works, And that my soul knows very well. My frame was not hidden from You, When I was made in secret, And skillfully wrought in the lowest parts of the earth. Your eyes saw my substance, being yet unformed. And **in Your book they all were written, The days fashioned for me,** When as yet there were none of them"* (Psalm 139:13–16, emphasis added).

God's plan for your life will be found where you experience pleasure and where you experience His pleasure in you.

"Be aware of your strengths. When you teach, do people listen? When you lead, do people follow? When you administer, do things improve? Where are you most productive? Identify your strengths, and then—this is important—major in them. Take a few irons out of the fire so this one can get hot. Failing to focus on our strengths may prevent us from accomplishing the unique tasks God has called us to do."[68]

The body of Christ must recognize that God never intended that a spiritual leader be all things to all people. And spiritual leaders must recognize that the church was not intended to fulfill his or her ministry dreams. The role of the five-fold ministry is to equip each person to serve in his or her God-assigned role (Ephesians 4:7–13). (The five-fold ministers may function in the church or in the marketplace). When people are in their proper positions, their hearts will be fulfilled, but even more importantly, God's dreams will begin to happen. The "needs" will be meet because the body of Christ is functioning as a human body. Today "a seeing eye" may be trying to serve as a "hearing ear" because of a need to listen to people's troubles (counseling). The problem is that the eye isn't created to hear and will "burn out" serving as an ear. God has a plan and purpose for every congregation. I know too many Christians who are burned out from serving in the wrong places because they were "gifted" and there were needs to be met. We need to pray in the right people and create avenues so the body can serve according to who God created each member to be.

God designed each of us with unique motivations, giftings, and desires. We are happiest when we are moving in those giftings and desires. Each Christian should assess these areas, especially leaders, since anointing flows from them to the followers. Jamie Buckingham describes how the ten elders in the Tabernacle Church in Melbourne submitted themselves to a process. They took a series of vocational tests to discover their motivational gifts. Then they individually prayed, focusing on the questions: "What is the best contribution I can make to the Body of Christ? What are the real desires of my heart? What is God telling me to do with my life?" Then they shared. "A lot of interesting things came to the surface during those few days in the beach cabin. We found we had asked each other to do certain things in order to fill needs rather than because it was God's highest will for the individual. We had not been sensitive to each other's dreams. All of us had assumed responsibilities greater than our capabilities. One of the men finally put his finger on the problem. 'The question,' he said, 'is what are we willing to quit in order to do those things God is asking us to do? The problem is how to differentiate between what I can do and what I am *supposed to do*.' "[69] Those who achieve in God's kingdom or the world's kingdom are able to focus on what they need to do. They eliminate the peripheral activities. They concentrate on first things first, and second things second. Do you know what God wants you to do first? How about second? Then do it with all your heart!

Serving by pouring out our lives for God is critical for our spiritual, emotional, and physical health. It allows us to be like the Sea of Galilee, where water pours into the Jordan River, rather than the Dead Sea, which receives the water of the Jordan but never gives out. Serving is God's weapon of choice in this world. Jesus demonstrated this in John 13 at the last supper prior to His death: *"If I then, your Lord and Teacher, have washed your feet, you also ought to wash one another's feet. For I have given you an example, that you should do as I have done to you. Most assuredly, I say to you, a servant is not greater than his master; nor is he who is sent greater than he who sent him"* (John 13:14–16). Jesus expected us to be servants of one another. No task is too low for us. We need to hear the voice of God calling us to serve Him and His people (whether or not they know Jesus). If you are called as a leader, God may ask you to clean someone's house. It may not be part of your vision, but it may be part of your calling to follow Jesus as a servant. Are you willing?

Yet we are not always called to serve the structure of the church. Sometimes the place of our ministry is where we work or live—just as a pastor or missionary serves where he works. Our fulltime ministry is where we are serving the purposes of God. I am in fulltime ministry working as a leader in senior management at an office as much as I was when I served as a missionary.

The perceptions of leaders and followers are different, whether in the business world or the church world. "When looking ahead and focusing on a new direction, leaders anticipate the road ahead. We major on reasons for change. We formulate a logical process for pursuing and promoting change. Leaders operate as the initiators of change, not the subjects of it. Leadership terminology involves words such as *challenge, opportunity, faith, excitement, benefits, new, radical, effective, productive, power, warfare, relevance, new level, and dimension.*"[70] Leaders help people and organizations become transformed into their God-intended purposes. A leader has a father's or mother's heart for people, to teach and mentor them to be all they can be in God and before God. In my latest job, I have been able to help set up the standards, processes, and culture of a start-up company—to help establish the foundation. Many of the consultants have expressed how much they would like to work on one of my projects. This is partly because I mentor and train them to be the best they can be. I use God's principles to manage projects and decide which ones to propose. Many of the business development people request me to be the Engagement Manager for their projects. It has been fulfilling.

Just like the wise virgins, we need to know when to say "no" to a good cause. We cannot meet every need in the world or the church. But some of us try. In the end, we run out of fuel (oil) and burn out. We need to have a sane estimation of our abilities and calling and stick to them. A Messiah complex says, "Unless I rise up and take on this task, God's Kingdom will fall apart and I will be responsible." It may sound funny in print. Yet subtly each of thinks this way at times. God expects us to serve where He asks us to serve, but not answer every need in the church or the world around us. Even Jesus said "No" occasionally. Like Mary, He chose the good part. I have found it a discipline to say "No." It is often hard to displease people, especially a leader. We are also called to let our yes be yes, and our no be no (Matthew 5:37). If you make a commitment, it is important to complete it. The time to ask if a task is right for you is when the original question comes, not when you are burning out from too many activities. The key is not to forget the priority of time with God in the secret place. We need to abide in the vine. If we do not let God prune the extra activities, we may grow lots of beautiful leaves but have no fruit that remains.

Apostolic Perseverance

Abraham Lincoln served as president through one of the darkest, dare I say wilderness, times for America. He lead the nation through a devastating civil war and the emancipation of the slaves. How was he prepared for this task? He walked through a number of disappointments. He had two business failures. He won one election, but lost eight! His fiancé died. He experienced a mental breakdown. Finally against all odds, he was elected president of the United States in 1860. He persevered in spite of all his disappointments.

Paul knew where he was called to serve. Was his call easy? No, not really. *"From the Jews five times I received forty stripes minus one. Three times I was beaten with rods; once I was stoned; three times I was shipwrecked; a night and a day I have been in the deep; in journeys often, in perils of waters, in perils of robbers, in perils of my own countrymen, in perils of the Gentiles, in perils in the city, in perils in the wilderness, in perils in the sea, in perils among false brethren; in weariness and toil, in sleeplessness often, in hunger and thirst, in fastings often, in cold and nakedness—besides the other things, what comes upon me daily: my deep concern for all the churches"* (2 Corinthians 11:24–28). Talk about stress and burnout! Yet Paul persevered, because he knew he was doing what God called him to do. Feeling the love and pleasure of God sustained him through the hard times. Like Jesus, he knew the joy set before him.

Are you desperate for God? Can you persevere through the hard times?

Strands of Pearls

God brings beauty to our lives in unique ways—His ways. He takes the irritants in our lives and turns them into pearls. But there is no guarantee that a pearl will be created from these irritants. Occasionally, an oyster will excrete the irritant (pass on the trial) and so a pearl is not formed. Sometimes the pearl is of lesser beauty and quality because the process was sped up or not properly applied. Listen carefully to how a pearl is formed to hear God's heart for you as the bride.

An Oyster's Life

Oysters are interesting animals. They are ugly to the eye and don't really do anything. One will attach itself to one place and grow there. Oysters are invertebrates and belong to the bivalve mollusk group. So in addition to be boring, they have no backbone! On the other hand, they are as old as creation and now live in many parts of the world in slightly different variations in size and color. There are over four hundred different species of oysters today.[71]

Unlike most bivalves, the two halves of an oyster's shell are different. The bottom shell is hollowed out to accommodate the oyster's body. The top half is thinner and flatter and forms the "roof." It has a very strong adductor muscle to keep the shell closed when protection is needed. When it is relaxed, it opens its shell and feeds on tiny plants and animals floating by. The mantle is a critical outer layer of the oyster's body. It secretes layer after layer of calcite to form the layer effect on the oyster's shell. When an irritating particle, such as a grain of sand or a parasite, gets caught in the shell, it isolates the irritant by forming one layer of conchiolin and several layers of nacre over it. Once it starts forming, it never stops. This is how a pearl is formed.

Pearls

Pearls are organic gems that are renowned for their beauty. Since pearls come from living organisms, each one is unique. They come in many colors, sizes, and shapes. It takes up to ten years for a six-millimeter pearl to form. Pearls today come in three varieties. Natural pearls are formed by nature in either the sea or fresh water. Cultured pearls come from "seeds" placed in the oysters by man so the pearls can be harvested years later. A seed can be an oyster shell or another irritant that is covered in another oyster's mantle. The beauty and rarity of a natural pearl comes from its uniqueness. Very rarely is it perfectly round. "The pearl itself is something that would never have been created without adversity and struggle! And perhaps even more important, whether or not there will be a pearl at all, and the quality and beauty of the pearl, depends upon what the individual mollusk does to deal with the situation; not all mollusks in the same situation create a pearl, and of those that do, not all create something beautiful."[72] Many pearls today are of such poor quality that they will lose their luster in just months and will not survive the test of time.

Six factors that affect a pearl's value and quality are:[73]

- **Luster and orient**. Luster is the result of rays of light traveling through the numerous layers of nacre and being reflected back from **within** the pearl. Some might describe it as "shine within depth." Orient is the iridescent quality of the pearl when sufficient layers of nacre have been built up.
- **Nacre thickness and quality**. Nacre is made of crystals of calcium carbonate, and is built up year upon year. It is the correct alignment of the crystals forming a prismatic effect that causes the pearl's iridescence. The thicker the nacre and the more perfectly aligned the crystals, the greater the beauty and cost of the pearl. The greatest beauty comes from being under pressure

for the greatest number of years!
- **Color**. Pearls come in many colors, including silvery white, cream, pink, and black. The body color is the primary color, such as white. The overtone will give it a unique tint, such as pink, green, or blue. The rarer the color, the more costly the pearl.
- **Surface perfection**. A pearl is never perfect. The highest quality pearls are those with the least visible blemishes, such as blisters, spots, or cracks.
- **Shape**. Pearls are categorized into spherical (round), symmetrical (teardrop), and baroque (irregular) shapes. Pearls come in all shapes and sizes.
- **Size**. Natural pearls are sold by weight. Cultured pearls are sold by millimeter size.

Our Pearls

In the Bible, pearls are metaphors for things of great value. Jesus describes each of us as the pearl of great price for whom He gave His life (Matthew 13:46). In the New American Standard Bible, acquisition of wisdom is considered greater than pearls (Job 28:18). In the New Jerusalem, each gate is a single huge pearl (Revelation 21:21). The gates represent the twelve tribes of Israel. Pearls can also stand for gross extravagance as in the description of the whore of Babylon who traffics in pearls and other gems (Revelation 17:4 and 18:12).

God uses the irritants in our lives to produce pearls. We must allow God to finish the process so that the end result will be gorgeous pearls that will endure the test of time! Over time, our difficulties and disappointments become pearls that God carefully hand knots into strands for a pearl necklace to adorn the bride. God wants us to shine from within with His light and be submitted to having our imperfections smoothed out. He also wants each of our lives and ministries to be unique in shape and size. It is only when we recognize that the painful areas become our greatest strengths that we know that we are beautiful in God's eyes. In many cultures, pearls are given to adorn a bride on her wedding day to demonstrate her worth.

After a season in the wilderness ends, one enters into a new identity and destiny. It is the blessing after the wrestling. But God likes us to have reminders of those seasons. Sometimes they are called "memorial stones" or "stones of remembrance" (Exodus 28:12 and Joshua 4:3). Here I am using the analogy of pearls as stones of remembrance.

The pearl represents the wisdom and beauty in our lives that have developed by walking with God through many trials.

In Matthew 7:6, Jesus tells us not to cast our pearls before swine. The pearl represents the wisdom and beauty in our lives that have developed by walking with God through many trials. Also, it is the oil in our lamps in the parable of the Ten Virgins. It is our individual relationship history with God. It is not something to be shared lightly, even when we are entreated by others who say the light is going out in their lamps. We need to value these treasures that God has worked into the fabric of our beings with reverence.

Pearls are also the fruit described in Galatians 5:22–23: *"But the fruit of the Spirit is love, joy, peace, longsuffering, kindness, goodness, faithfulness, gentleness, self-control."* The fruit of the Spirit comes by perseverance in God's process: *"We also glory in tribulations, knowing that tribulation produces perseverance; and perseverance, character; and character, hope. Now hope does not disappoint, because the love of God has been poured out in our hearts by the Holy Spirit who was given to us"* (Romans 5:3–5).

Looking for the Bridegroom

Let's be honest—why would anyone be willing to go through the process? Yes, the fruit and character building are great, but the process is painful! We do it for the same reason Jesus endured the cross: *"Looking unto Jesus, the **author and finisher of our faith**, who **for the joy that was set before Him endured the cross, despising the shame**, and has sat down at **the right hand of the throne of God**. For consider Him who endured such hostility from sinners against Himself, lest you become weary and discouraged in your souls"* (Hebrews 12:2–3, emphasis added). Jesus kept His eyes on the joy before Him. He had dove eyes for the Father. It helped Him endure the process of the cross without getting discouraged.

We want to focus on Jesus in the secret place while we wait for his return:

- Worship him deeply for who He is, not just what He has done for us. This can be done in music and dance, but also in lifestyle.
- Do what we see Him doing and saying. This means listening and watching, and then obeying.
- Read scriptures for a revelation of who He is, not just looking for doctrine, a teaching, or even revelation.
- Pray, "Lord, show me Your heart and my heart." Ask what's on His mind and heart.
- Ask Him to sing over you songs of deliverance (Zephaniah 3:17).
- Feed the fire on the altar in your heart so it is flaming brightly and never goes out (Leviticus 6:12–13, Revelation 8:3–4).
- Live a contagious life that will make others divinely jealous, so they will want to know God (Romans 11:11).
- Recognize that our reward is coming (Revelation 22:12–17).
- Choose dove eyes that only look to the bridegroom, Jesus (Song of Solomon 1:15).

Let's examine some of the benefits of letting God complete the process of the wilderness.

Restoration

In chapter 42, Job finally receives restoration. God gave him twice as much as he had before. His brothers, sisters, and friends came and consoled him for the adversity he experienced. They even brought him gold and silver! His health was restored. His latter days were blessed more than the beginning. He was able to see four generations of his family. The second set of children (seven sons and three daughters) was born in this restoration period and had more godly characters than the first set.

Some of the keys to his restoration were the waiting for the fullness of time, acknowledging that God **will** work **all** of His purposes, worshipping, interceding for his friends, and receiving the Lord's acceptance. Remember that the blessing or restoration is to be the end of the season of wrestling.

When restitution is made in the Bible, it is always increased, multiplied, or improved. In the *Torah*, a person is required to restore double what he stole: *"If the thief is found, he shall pay double"* (Exodus 22:7). *"Return to the stronghold, You prisoners of hope. Even today I declare That I will restore double to you"* (Zechariah 9:12). Even Babylon will be repaid double for her injustices (Revelation 18:6).

Joseph is another example of a person of God who was forsaken, falsely accused, forgotten, and then restored (Genesis 37–46). God tempered him in the furnace of affliction to be in a position to deliver the nations of Egypt and Israel at a critical hour. The scriptures never indicate that he was bitter through his circumstances.

Restoration simply means life! Moses told the people, *"**Choose life**, that both you and your descendants may live; **that you may love the LORD your God**, that you may **obey His voice**, and that you may **cling to Him**, for **He is your life** and the length of your days"* (Deuteronomy 30:19–20, emphasis added). Paul said, *"When **Christ who is our life** appears, then you also will appear with Him in glory"* (Colossians 3:4, emphasis added). Just as Jesus was dead and was resurrected to life eternal, so God longs to take us from our spiritually dead states and bring us to eternal life. He wants to take our hearts of stone and replace them with hearts of flesh. It is then that we will be restored to an even better relationship with God than Adam and Eve had in Eden. Restoration is establishing something greater than the original. It is life more abundantly!

Why does God restore? He does it for His own glory (John 9:3). He wants a testimony passed on to the next generation as an inheritance, so they can go even further in God. Almost every breakthrough in my life has come out of suffering. The increase in the anointing comes from the oil press bringing forth oil from the former flesh. God knows our hearts. When He sees how we respond in the hard place, He knows He can trust us with greater anointing. He also desires us to see our own hearts of faithfulness and persever- ance under the most difficult of circumstances. He wants us to know our hearts are leaning toward God and to see His pleasure in it.

I know I have entered a season of restoration. I believe God is restoring what the enemy stole and what was burned on the altars.

Wisdom

Job 28:12–28 is a discourse asking, *"Where can wisdom be found? And where is the place of understanding? Man does not know its value."* Although man can find gold and gems in the earth, he cannot find wisdom. Wisdom is of far more value than the earth's treasures. *"It is hidden from the eyes of all living.... [Only]* ***God understands its way****, And He knows its place.... He saw wisdom and declared it; He prepared it, indeed, He searched it out. And* ***to man He said, 'Behold, the fear of the Lord, that is wisdom, And to depart from evil is understanding'"*** (emphasis added). The fear of the Lord is the beginning of wisdom. It is as we press in to know (*yada*) God that wisdom comes to our lives.

Hebrew has at least five words for wisdom. Greek has only one. The five Hebrew words demonstrate the nuances of different types of wisdom and its value in God's economy. Knowledge is knowing the facts, and wisdom is knowing how to apply the facts. Wisdom can be equated with strategy.

God provides us with wisdom that equips us with the creativity and skills to perform the tasks before us, whether in the world or the church. Both can advance the Kingdom of God: *"See, the LORD has called by name Bezalel the son of Uri, the son of Hur, of the tribe of Judah; and* ***He has filled him with the Spirit of God, in wisdom and understanding, in knowledge and all manner of workmanship, to design artistic works****, to work in gold and silver and bronze, in cutting jewels for setting, in carving wood, and to work in all manner of artistic workmanship. And* ***He has put in his heart the ability to teach****, in him and Aholiab the son of Ahisamach, of the tribe of Dan. He has* ***filled them with skill to do all manner of work*** *of the engraver and the designer and the tapestry maker, in blue, purple, and scarlet thread, and fine linen, and of the weaver— those who do every work and those who design artistic works"*

(Exodus 35:30–35, emphasis added).

"Joseph was then given wisdom to apply to Pharaoh's dream, which application was the proper course of action. It flowed out of him just like the interpretation had, but it came by unction of the Holy Spirit as opposed to just receiving divine information, because the application requires not just divine wisdom, but divine timing as well.... Application is also the place where the spiritual and natural will often meet. In this case, after Joseph received the spiritual revelation about the famine, physical action had to be added to the equation in order to get the job done. Many natural giftings and talents, including Joseph's, had to be put to work storing and administering."[74] We must use wisdom to act on a vision or strategy so it will become a reality. Joshua *"was full of the spirit of wisdom, for Moses had laid his hands on him"* (Deuteronomy 34:9). Solomon was renowned throughout the earth for his wisdom (1 Kings 10:24).

Proverbs 4 discusses the benefits of following wisdom's ways: *"'**Get wisdom!** Get understanding! Do not forget, nor turn away from the words of my mouth. Do not forsake her, and **she will preserve you**; Love her, and she will keep you. **Wisdom is the principal thing**; therefore get wisdom. And in all your getting, get understanding. Exalt her, and **she will promote you**; **She will bring you honor**, when you embrace her. **She will place on your head an ornament of grace; A crown of glory she will deliver to you.**' Hear, my son, and receive my sayings, and the years of your life will be many. I have taught you in the way of wisdom; I have led you in right paths. **When you walk, your steps will not be hindered**, And **when you run, you will not stumble**. Take firm hold of instruction, do not let go; **Keep her, for she is your life"** (Proverbs 4:5–13, emphasis added).

Power

God is about to release great power on the earth in signs and wonders. The generation on the earth when Jesus returns will see many supernatural things, more than Israel saw in Moses' time or the Apostles saw in the time of Jesus. Power is not for personal glory or gain, but for the glory of God. *"And it shall come to pass afterward That I will pour out My Spirit on all flesh; Your sons and* *your daughters **shall prophesy**, Your old men shall **dream dreams**, Your young men shall **see visions**. And also on My menservants and on My maidservants I will pour out My Spirit in those days. And **I will show wonders in the heavens and in the earth**: Blood and fire and pillars of smoke. The sun shall be turned into darkness, And the moon into blood, **Before the coming of the great and awesome day of the LORD**. And it shall come to pass That whoever calls on the name of the LORD Shall be saved. For in Mount Zion and in Jerusalem there shall be deliverance, As the LORD has said, Among the remnant whom the LORD calls"* (Joel 2:28–32, emphasis added).

When we are truly an extension of Jesus' heart, I believe the miracles will happen supernaturally naturally.

Signs and wonders will be tied to the heart of the Father and the compassion of Jesus. It is only when we have been transformed into the image of Jesus **and** have His heart that He can trust us with the true power and authority of the Kingdom. Compassion for people is one of the fruits from intimacy with Jesus. There are twelve references in the synoptic Gospels demonstrating Jesus' compassion on the multitudes or an individual. *"So Jesus had compassion and touched their eyes. And immediately their eyes received sight, and they followed Him"* (Matthew 20:34). Our hearts need to be filled with the Father's love, so we move out of compassion to see the multitudes healed. During worship, I saw Jesus carry the heart of individuals to His heart. As He placed each heart within His heart it disappeared in the beauty of His heartbeat. Then with a smile on His face, He took a piece of His heart and carried it down to each of us. It was precious. When we are truly an extension of Jesus' heart, I believe the miracles will happen supernaturally naturally.

What we thought was great power before is nothing compared to what we will see. *"Believe Me that **I am in the Father and the Father in Me**, or else believe Me for the sake of the works themselves. Most assuredly, I say to you, he who believes in Me, **the** *works that I do he will do also; and greater works than these he will do, because I go to My Father. And whatever you ask in My name, that I will do, that the Father may be glorified in the Son. If you ask anything in My name, I will do it"* (John 14:11–14, emphasis added). The miracles will not be about confirming our ministries or doctrines. They will be for glorifying the Father in Jesus. *"And He said to them, 'It is not for you to know times or seasons which the Father has put in His own authority. But you shall receive power when the Holy Spirit has come upon you; and you shall be witnesses to Me in Jerusalem, and in all Judea and Samaria, and to the end of the earth'"* (Acts 1:7–8, emphasis added). We are to receive the power of the Holy Spirit so we can be witnesses to who Jesus is. We can only fully witness to Him when we know (*yada*) Him rather than just know about His acts. The Father is the only one who knows the time and season when the bride will know Him that completely.

What we call the spirit, John G. Lake called the soul. He lived from 1870 to 1935. "Beloved, your soul will never demonstrate the power of God in any appreciable degree until your soul conceives and understands the real vision of the Christ of God, whereby He knew that through union with the living God His soul became the creative power through which He took possession of the power of God and applied it to the needs of His own soul, and the needs of other lives."[75] God used John G. Lake in many miraculous healings and deliverances. He knew the power of God. But even more importantly, he knew and believed the living God. One of my favorite stories is how he used a powerful x–ray machine to prove the power of God.[76]

One of the greatest hindrances to moving into signs and wonders is a religious, political spirit that pridefully wants to look and act right. Some believe that confidence in religious activities like Bible reading, prayer, or fasting is passion for Jesus. But our confidence is to be in a living God who has likes, dislikes, and present priorities. We need to love the author more than the book! 1 Corinthians 3 talks about defiling the body of Christ by strife and divisions. Often it is the "wise" or those in authority who defile the body with a critical orientation and arrogant knowledge. He or she will say, directly or indirectly, "I really know what is right" or "We are on the cutting edge." We are to esteem others better than ourselves. Religious spirits emphasize I, my church, or my pastor is better. Self-righteousness draws on a spirit of pride. It is also blindness of heart. A religious spirit will exaggerate what God did. A religious spirit has something to lose if you don't agree. Paul had a progressive recognition of his sin until he became the "chief of sinners." He had no trace of pride or self-righteousness left. God is calling us to be authentic at every level. The time for hiding behind façades or pretending that everything is rosy are over. God wants us to be honest with ourselves, others, and Him so He can move in our hearts. Pride doesn't allow Him to move in power. God wants people with leaning hearts who look to Him to see what He is seeing and doing **before** He will release the full power. But it is coming!

Just as in the time of Moses and the Apostles, the false signs and wonders are also coming. The rise of occultic activities will also raise up the false "miraculous." People are hungry for the supernatural. We need to have the real supernatural so we can point them to the compassionate heart of Jesus. Because of the release of lawlessness, many in this generation will be "dead" and will need to see God's resurrection power.

Purity

Merriam-Webster defines "pure" as "unmixed with any other matter ... or free from what weakens or pollutes...."[77] God is looking for a bride who is made of the same substance He is, without any pollutants mixed in. This is a stretch for most of us, as we still have the ways of the world in our lives. Just like the clay had to go through a slip and the gold needed to be refined, so our lives need to be processed for purity. Everything in the tabernacle and temple needed to be "pure," whether it was gold, oil, or frankincense. *"All the ways of a man are pure in his own eyes, But the LORD weighs the spirits. Commit your works to the LORD, and your thoughts will be established"* (Proverbs 16:2–3).

*"Husbands, love your wives, just as Christ also loved the church and gave Himself for her, that **He might sanctify and cleanse her with the washing of water by the word**, that He might present her to Himself **a glorious church, not having spot or wrinkle** or any such thing, but that she should be **holy and without blemish**"* (Ephesians

5:25–27, emphasis added). God provides the Bible and His love as primary ways to bring forth purity in the bride. When we know that we are loved and we let God deal with the issues of our lives through repentance and changing priorities, we come forth as the fragrance of spring. We will be a bride without spot or wrinkle.

Below are some of the benefits of purity and consecration:

- *He who loves purity of heart And has grace on his lips, The king will be his friend* (Proverbs 22:11). We get to be his friend.
- *With the pure You will show Yourself pure; And with the devious You will show Yourself shrewd* (Psalm 18:26). This scripture is found five times through the Bible.
- Perhaps most importantly, *Blessed are the pure in heart, For they shall see God* (Matthew 5:8).

I want to see God—how about you?

Humility

One of the keys in Rick Joyner's *The Final Quest* is receiving the mantle of humility, which appears plain and insignificant. "You are the dreaded champions, the sons and daughters of the King. He wore the same mantle when He walked on this earth. As long as you are clothed in that, there is no power in heaven or earth that can stand before you. Everyone in heaven and hell recognizes that mantle. We are indeed His servants but He abides in you, and you are clothed in His grace."[78] Then when Rick has the revelation at the White Throne judgment, Jesus speaks. "Those who will sit here will be know to have two things: they will wear the mantle of humility and they will have My likeness. You now have the mantle. If you can keep it and do not lose it in the battle, when you return you will also have My likeness. Then you will be worthy to sit with these, because I have made you worthy. All authority and power has been given to Me, and I alone can wield it. You will prevail, and you will be trusted with My authority only when you have come to fully abide in Me."[79]

Let's examine some of the scriptures on humility.

"Likewise you younger people, submit yourselves to your elders.

*Yes, all of you be submissive to one another, and **be clothed with humility**, for 'God resists the proud, But gives grace to the humble.' Therefore **humble yourselves under the mighty hand of God, that He may exalt you in due time, casting all your care upon Him**, for He cares for you. **Be sober, be vigilant;** because your adversary the devil walks about like a roaring lion, seeking whom he may devour"* (1 Peter 5:5–8 and James 4:6, emphasis added). We must ask God to clothe us with humility; it is not a garment we put on ourselves. God will give us humility as we submit ourselves to Him and one to another. We choose to humble ourselves, and then God extends grace to us. Choosing to humble ourselves takes a leaning heart that is dependent on God for all things.

*"The **fear of the LORD is the instruction of wisdom**, And **before honor is humility"*** (Proverbs 15:33, emphasis added). Fear of the Lord and wisdom are linked to humility.

*"**Seek the LORD,** all **you meek** of the earth, who have **upheld His justice. Seek righteousness, seek humility.** It may be **that you will be hidden In the day of the LORD's anger"*** (Zephaniah 2:3, emphasis added). The command is to seek the Lord and His righteousness and justice (not our own). As we seek the Lord and receive the cloak of humility, it will keep us hidden in the end times.

*"And a **servant of the Lord must not quarrel** but be gentle to all, **able to teach, patient, in humility correcting** those who are in opposition, if God perhaps will grant them repentance, so that they may know the truth, and that they may come to their senses and escape the snare of the devil, having been taken captive by him to do his will"* (2 Timothy 2:24–26, emphasis added). When we disagree with someone, Paul states we are not to quarrel, but patiently teach and correct in humility, not in anger.

*"Remind them **to be subject to rulers and authorities, to obey, to be ready for every good work, to speak evil of no one, to be peaceable, gentle, showing all humility to all men.** For we ourselves were also once foolish, disobedient, deceived, serving various lusts and pleasures, living in malice and envy, hateful and hating one another. But when the kindness and the love of God our Savior toward man appeared, not by works of righteousness which we have done, **but according to His mercy He saved us, through the washing of regeneration and renewing of the Holy Spirit, whom***

He poured out on us abundantly through Jesus Christ our Savior, that **having been justified** by His grace we should become heirs according to the hope of eternal life" (Titus 3:1–7, emphasis added). In all our dealings with people, we are to show humility, whether they have higher or lower stations in life. As I humbly recognize what God saved me from and how He regenerated me, then I (and you) will deal with all people in humility. Until we recognize, like Job, that we are little compared to God, we cannot receive the cloak of humility. There must be gratefulness for what He has done in our lives!

"**If** My people *who are called by My name* **will humble them-selves**, *and* **pray and seek My face**, *and* **turn from their wicked ways,** <u>*then*</u> *I will hear from heaven, and will forgive their sin and heal their land*" (2 Chronicles 7:14, emphasis added). This scripture is often quoted in prayer groups and churches. Immediately you see it is a conditional "if-then" statement. The "if" part is for people whom God calls "my people," those who have an intimate relationship with Him. The call is to humble ourselves, pray, seek His face (not His hand), and walk in repentance. These are all disciplines of forerunners. "Then" God will listen to our prayers, forgive us, and heal our land. These are critical in this day and hour!

Moses was trusted with executing God's judgment through signs and wonders. What does scripture say about him? *"Now the man Moses was very humble, more than all men who were on the face of the earth"* (Numbers 12:3). I suspect this had a great deal to do with why he was called to this role. This was a very different attitude from when he killed the Egyptian in anger and pride. What changed him? Spending forty years as a shepherd in the wilderness! God took the raw material in Moses and reshaped it on the backside of the desert. God gifted Moses with two wilderness experiences, one to shape his character and the other to lead Israel through. Was Moses perfect? No—from the glory cloud, God told him to speak to the rock for water to come forth. Instead, he struck the rock twice with his staff. He stopped leaning on God temporarily. Moses and Aaron paid a high price for this act of not believing and trusting. *"The LORD said to Moses and Aaron, '**Because you did not trust in me enough to honor me as holy in the sight of the Israelites,** you will not bring this community into the land I give them'"*

(Numbers 20:12, emphasis added). Moses died on Mt. Nebo in sight of the Promised Land (Deuteronomy 32:51). This puts the fear of God in me.

He humbled them to increase their hunger for Him so they might live by God's word and not their flesh.

In Deuteronomy chapter 8, Moses spoke to Israel, reminding them of what He did in the wilderness: *"And **you shall remember that the LORD your God led you** all the way these forty years **in the wilderness, to humble you and test you, to know what was in your heart, whether you would keep His commandments or not. So He humbled you, allowed you to hunger,** and fed you with manna which you did not know nor did your fathers know, that He might make you know that man shall not live by bread alone; **but man lives by every word that proceeds from the mouth of the LORD"*** (verses 2–3, emphasis added). The wilderness was to humble the Israelites. God was going to expose what was in their hearts to test whether they would follow in His ways. He humbled them to increase their hunger for Him so they might live by God's word and not their flesh.

The next test is coming out of the wilderness, into *"a good land, a land of brooks of water, of fountains and springs, that flow out of valleys and hills; a land of wheat and barley, of vines and fig trees and pomegranates, a land of olive oil and honey; a land in which you will eat bread without scarcity, in which you will lack nothing"* (verses 7–9). The test is, will you bless the Lord your God and remember His ways? Or will pride rise up and *"say in your heart, 'My power and the might of my hand have gained me this wealth'"* (verse 17)? Or will you remember *"the LORD your God, for it is He who gives you power to get wealth, that He may establish His covenant which He swore to your fathers, as it is this day"* (verse 18)? The test is: what will we do with God's abundance, Job's two-fold restoration? Will you remember God or be like Solomon and follow after the idol of mammon and other gods? It is a very real question. God will continue to test our hearts. He needs to know we can handle His abundance in His ways.

From Glory to Glory

*"Nevertheless **when one turns to the Lord**, the veil is taken away. Now the Lord is the Spirit; and **where the Spirit of the Lord is, there is liberty**. But we all, with unveiled face, **beholding as in a mirror the glory of the Lord**, are being transformed into the same image from glory to glory, just as by the Spirit of the Lord"* (2 Corinthians 3:16–18, emphasis added).

*"After these things I looked, and behold, a door standing open in heaven. And the first voice which I heard was like a trumpet speaking with me, saying, '**Come up here, and I will show you things which must take place after this.'** Immediately I was in the Spirit; and behold, a throne set in heaven, and One sat on the throne"* (Revelation 4:1–2, emphasis added).

When the veil begins to come off our hearts, we see the Lord more and more. As we behold the glory of the Lord with greater intensity, we are transformed to mirror that glory to others. A liberty to follow after Jesus comes that frees us from the expectations of others, even in the church. This is a continuous process so that we go from one glory realm to another on hind's feet. Jesus is extending the invitation "come up here" so that He can show us things we haven't seen before—the glory realm.

Hinds' Feet in High Places

As we long deeply with our whole hearts, minds, and souls for God, He makes our way perfect. He gives us hind's feet to leap on The Rock in the high places of God. He teaches us to walk in His perfect ways so we can run and not be weary. But there must be a hunger and thirst, almost a desperation in our soul, to go to the high places and persevere until we reach them.

> *"As the deer pants for the water brooks, So pants my soul for You, O God. My soul thirsts for God, for the living God. When shall I come and appear before God?"* (Psalm 42:1–2, emphasis added).

> *"For who is God, except the LORD? And who is a rock, except our God? It is God who arms me with strength, And makes my way perfect. He makes my feet like the feet of deer, And sets me on my high places"* (Psalm 18:31–33, emphasis added).

> *"Though the fig tree may not blossom, Nor fruit be on the vines; Though the labor of the olive may fail, And the fields yield no food; Though the flock may be cut off from the fold, And there be no herd in the stalls—Yet I will rejoice in the LORD, I will joy in the God of my salvation. The LORD God is my strength; He will make my feet like deer's feet, And He will make me walk on my high hills"* (Habakkuk 3:17–19, emphasis added).

Like Much-Afraid in Hannah Hurnard's *Hind's Feet in High Places*, we must stumble slowly up the lower hills before coming to the High Places. We must meet and overcome fear, pride, loneliness, resentment, and laying down our will daily. Much-Afraid learned to build altars when she needed to lay down her will or desires on her path to the High Places. Each time the fire of the sacrifice died down an ordinary looking stone was left behind in the ashes. Much-Afraid is renamed "Grace and Glory" in the High Places.

After that he said, "give me the bag of stones of

remembrance that you have gathered on your journey, Grace and Glory."

She took it out and passed it to him and then he bade her hold out her hands. On doing so, he opened the little purse and emptied the contents into her hands. Then she gasped again with bewilderment and delight, for instead of the common, ugly stones she had gathered from the altars along the way, there fell into her hands a heap of glorious, sparkling jewels, very precious and very beautiful. As she stood there, half-dazzled by the glory of the flashing gems, she saw in his hand a circlet of pure gold.

"O thou who wast afflicted, tossed with tempest and not comforted," he said, "behold I lay thy stones with fair colors."

First he picked out of her hand one of the biggest, and most beautiful of the stones—a sapphire, shining like the pavement of heaven, and set it in the center of the golden circlet. Then, taking a fiery, blood red ruby, he set it on the side of the sapphire and an emerald on the other. After that he took the other stones—twelve in all—and arranged them on the circlet, then set it on her forehead.

At that moment Grace and Glory remembered the cave in which she had sheltered from the floods, and how nearly she had succumbed to the temptation to discard as worthless those stones which shone in glory and splendor in the crown upon her head. She remembered, too, the words which had sounded in her ears and had restrained her, "Hold fast that thou hast, that no man take thy crown." Supposing she had thrown them away, discarded her trust in his promises, had gone back on her surrenders to his will? There could have been no jewels to his praise and glory, and no crown for her to wear.

She marveled at the grace and love and tenderness and patience which had led and trained and guarded and kept poor faltering Much-Afraid, which had not allowed her to turn back, and which now changed all her trials into glory.[80]

There **is** a price to be paid to reach the high places. The high places surround the hottest deserts. When we willingly submit to the wilderness experience we arise to the high places of God. The price is worth all we have in this life! We can't even begin to understand the jewels we receive in the process. It is only when we can see from God's heavenly perspective that we begin to understand how precious and beautiful we are to Him. Then He encourages us to stretch beyond our comfort zones by taking longer and higher leaps so we can attain even higher places in Him. We climb the stairs of heaven. As we begin to have a heavenly perspective and walk in the glory realm, the spiritual realm of God can break into the natural realm with miracles. This is when the world as we know it will begin to be transformed into the kingdom of our God.

*"Then the **eyes of the blind shall be opened**, And the **ears of the deaf shall be unstopped**. Then the **lame shall leap like a deer**, And the **tongue of the dumb sing**. For **waters shall burst forth in the wilderness**, And **streams in the desert**. The parched ground shall become a pool, And the thirsty land springs of water; In the habitation of jackals, where each lay, There shall be grass with reeds and rushes. A highway shall be there, and a road, And it shall be called the **Highway of Holiness**"* (Isaiah 35:5–8, emphasis added). The high places are the Highway of Holiness. When we walk in His ways in the wilderness, living waters will burst forth from us so the supernatural miracles of God will break forth. Hallelujah!

But as Moses found out, the high places can be treacherous. We must maintain a high level of trust and obedience in God so we know exactly where to place our feet on His path. Deer have an uncanny ability to navigate up steep, rocky slopes. They use rocks to climb, much as a human would use fingers to grab hold of the next rock while rock climbing. What is amazing is how quickly deer navigate the slopes. I sometimes watched them on the Rockies. That is why God trains us in the wilderness.

What are some of the characteristics of the hind leaping in the High Places?

Glory

Much-Afraid's character, as represented by her name, is transformed into Grace and Glory. She receives a crown of glory that does not fade away (1 Peter 5:4). Scripture says, *"In that day the LORD of hosts will be For a crown of glory and a diadem of beauty To the remnant of His people"* (Isaiah 28:5); and *"You shall also be a crown of glory In the hand of the LORD, And a royal diadem In the hand of your God"* (Isaiah 62:3). So we will crown God, and He will crown us. This sounds like a mutual love affair. Wisdom will deliver to us a crown of glory as an ornament of grace (Proverbs 4:9 and 16:31). Glory is the restoration of those who were forced by the enemy to hide in shame.

> *"And he* [Moses] *said, 'Please, **show me Your glory.'** Then He said, **'I will make all My goodness pass before you**, and **I will proclaim the name of the LORD** before you. **I will be gracious** to whom I will be gracious, and **I will have compassion** on whom I will have compassion.' But He said, 'You cannot see My face; for no man shall see Me, and live.'"* (Exodus 33:18–20, emphasis added).

Moses asked God as a friend, "Show me Your glory!" How often have we asked God to show us His glory? God's answer used to surprise me: "I will have ALL My goodness, graciousness, and compassion pass before you, and I will proclaim My name and character before you." That wasn't what I expected. I expected the *shekinah* glory to come down! God's ways aren't our ways. So His glory, as well as His signs and wonders, are tied to His character of compassion. How often have we missed His glory by looking for the wrong things?

The glory realm is when we enter eternity while still being on the earth. It is a revelation of God Himself.

The primary meaning of glory (*kabod*) in Hebrew is a weightiness. It is the beauty, power, and honor of God, the part of His character that emphasizes His greatness and authority. The glory realm is when we enter eternity while still being on the earth. It is a revelation of God Himself. Glory is a tangible substance which can be seen with our natural eyes as well as our spiritual eyes. We see the glory when we have been through the fire, and then others will see His glory in us.

In *The Final Quest,* Rick Joyner understands that our healed wounds transform us for His glory:

> I looked at the old eagle, and for the first time I noticed the scars amid his torn and broken feathers. However, they were not ugly, but were lined with gold that was somehow not metal, but rather flesh and feathers. Then I could see that it was from this gold that gave off the glory that emanated from the eagle making his presence awesome.
>
> "Why did I not see this before?" I inquired.
>
> "Until you have beheld and appreciated the depths of salvation, you cannot see the glory that comes from suffering for the sake of the gospel. Once you have seen it, you are ready for the tests that will release the highest levels of spiritual authority into your life. These scars are the glory that we will carry forever. This is why even the wounds our Lord suffered are with Him in heaven. You can still see His wounds, and the wounds that all His chosen ones have taken for His sake. These are the medals of honor in heaven. All who carry them love God and His truth more than their own lives. These are the ones who followed the lamb wherever He went, being willing to suffer for the sake of truth, righteousness, and the salvation of men. True leaders of His people, who carry genuine spiritual authority, must have first proven their devotion this way."[81]

Yada of the Glory

The World Prayer Center in Colorado Springs has a huge globe in front of the windows through which one can look out on the Rockies. One day as I was worshipping, God said to me, "Look at globe." The part facing me was the Pacific Ocean with no land visible, but only water. He spoke, "My glory **will** cover the earth as the waters cover the sea." What I was seeing was like the flood of Noah, but this time instead of water, it would be His glory that would bring both judgment (flood) and safety (the Ark). The flood of Noah shook the earth; God's glory will shake heaven and earth. His glory will so cover the earth that nothing in the natural realm will be able to stand.

- Isaiah 11:9–12—Knowledge of God: *"'They shall not hurt nor destroy in all My holy mountain, **For the earth shall be full of the knowledge of the LORD As the waters cover the sea**. And in that day there shall be a Root of Jesse, who shall stand as a banner to the people; For the Gentiles shall seek Him, and **His resting place shall be glorious**.' It shall come to pass in that day That the Lord shall set His hand again the second time To recover the remnant of His people who are left ... He will set up a banner for the nations, And will assemble the outcasts of Israel, And gather together the dispersed of Judah From the four corners of the earth"* (emphasis added). The word for knowledge in these verses is *da'at*, so it is an experiential knowledge. People will know God by their senses, perhaps from God's judgment.

- Habakkuk 2:14 — Knowledge of the glory of God: *"**For the earth will be filled With the knowledge of the glory of the LORD, As the waters cover the sea**"* (emphasis added). Here the word for knowledge is *yada*; it is an intimate knowledge of the glory. It is when people know God intimately that they will know His glory and protection.

- Numbers 14:20–23—Glory of God: *"Then the LORD said: 'I have pardoned, according to your word; but truly, as I live, all **the earth shall be filled with the glory of the LORD**—because all these **men who have seen My glory** and the signs which I did in Egypt and in the wilderness, and have **put Me to the test** now these ten times, and have **not heeded My voice**, they certainly **shall not see the land** of which I swore to their fathers, nor shall any of those who rejected Me see it'"* (emphasis added). Those who see the glory of God and are not changed will be judged. Knowledge of His glory brings a greater sense of His holiness, His "other-than-ness."

• Psalm 72:18–19—Glory of God: *"Blessed be the LORD God, the God of Israel, Who only does wondrous things! And blessed be His glorious name forever! And **let the whole earth be filled with His glory**"* (emphasis added). God's glory will be seen in His wondrous acts.

• Isaiah 40:5—Glory of God: ***"The glory of the LORD shall be revealed, And all flesh shall see it together;** For the mouth of the LORD has spoken"* (emphasis added). The time is coming when the glory of the Lord will not be seen only by individuals but corporately, by everyone on the earth, at the same time! No one will be able to deny it! This will happen after the voices of those prepared in the wilderness have come forth (Isaiah 40:3). It will release the great harvest.

"A great restoration of God's power and presence will cover the earth in the End Times. The people of God will enjoy the divine presence, beauty, and power of God in a way never before imagined. The glory of God will cover the earth as the waters cover the seas. And when the glory is manifested, the nations will look up to Jesus Christ, and multitudes upon multitudes will be saved in the greatest ingathering of souls in the history of mankind."[82]

Rest

After we have seen glimpses of the glory realm, rest will come to us. It is a deep peace in knowing who God is and what He is doing on the earth. There may not be a knowledge of the details, but the deep abiding trust of God rests upon us. We begin to see ourselves, others, and current events through the eyes of Jesus rather than from our limited earthly perspective. Last year my dad sent me a picture of the earth as seen at night from space. It is a very different perspective from what I see while driving down the highway in congested traffic. We need to have that sort of perspective.

We no longer need to appear "spiritual" or "super-Christian." God abiding with you becomes natural, a part of who you are. Sharing about the one you love best is easy. Your definition of who you are is defined by your relationship with God, not by what you do. It is true that you are more spiritual, but there is less of a need to demonstrate it. You are more naturally supernatural. When I started a new job, I felt I was to share God by who I was rather than by my words. I had comments from several people that I was quite spiritual, which opened the door to share what I believe. It happened naturally.

The need to perform acts of service for a church or for people is no longer a compulsion. It flows out of who you are. Some may feel you are falling away from God because you are "serving less" in their eyes. Yet the service God calls you to may be hidden from other believers. The pressure from peers to perform becomes difficult because you know what God is asking of you is different. Your delight becomes pleasing the Lord rather than a pastor or friends. *"Then I said, 'Behold, I come; In the scroll of the book it is written of me. I delight to do Your will, O my God, And Your law is within my heart'"* (Psalm 40:7–8, emphasis added). This is not God's permission to be lazy, but you serve how He has asked you to serve. All who know God must pour their lives into other vessels or they will die. It just may be in unorthodox ways. Rest comes when we enter into the perfect will of God. The new strength enables us to rise up above the problems on eagle's wings and run the race set before us. It is also a place where we receive strategies for the next season.

The intimacy that comes from the glory brings us out of hiding from God, ourselves, and other people. He frees us from our sin and our façades so we can live fully before Him in true love and oneness. We are authentic for the first time. As we walk with Him in oneness, He covers us with His righteousness. Righteousness is coming into agreement with His purposes on the earth.

Oneness

The glory realm and unity are tied very closely together. Does unity bring the glory or does the glory bring the unity?

Solomon assembled all the elders and people of Israel. They brought the Ark of the Covenant and the holy furnishings from the tabernacle up from the City of David to the temple. The sacrifices were too numerous to count. Then God... *"Indeed it came to pass, when the trumpeters and singers were as one, to make one sound to be heard in praising and thanking the LORD, and when they lifted up their voice with the trumpets and cymbals and instruments of music, and praised the LORD, saying: 'For He is good, For His mercy endures forever,' that the house, the house of the LORD, was filled with a cloud, so that the priests could not continue ministering because of the cloud; for the glory of the LORD filled the house of God"* (2 Chronicles 5:13–14, emphasis added).

When unity came between the instruments and singers—they were on the same divine chord proclaiming God's goodness and mercy—God filled the temple with his visible, tangible presence. No one could stand or minister, but waited in His presence. His goodness and glory are tied together.

God knows the power of unity, both in the flesh and in the spirit. The Tower of Babel (Genesis 11) is the story of a people of *"one language and one speech"* who with one will built a tower to make a name for themselves. *"And the LORD said, 'Indeed the people are one and they all have one language, and this is what they begin to do; now nothing that they propose to do will be withheld from them'"* (Genesis 11:6). Unity is powerful! On Pentecost, when they were in one accord (Acts 2:1), the Holy Spirit came to powerfully transform their lives and the world with tongues of fire. They were then able to continue in one accord (Acts 2:46). True community came out of unity in the spirit. God is calling us into unity with Him first, and the body of Christ second.

"Hear, O Israel: The LORD our God, the LORD is one! You shall love the LORD your God with all your heart, with all your soul, and with all your strength. And these words which I command you today shall be in your heart. You shall teach them diligently to your children, and shall talk of them when you sit in your house, when you walk by the way, when you lie down, and when you rise up" (Deuteronomy 6:4–8, emphasis added). The Hebrew word for Lord is *Elohim*, which is masculine and plural (three or more). God is one, yet three. "One" in Hebrew is *echad*. It means one, a unit, united, or unity, similar to the cords of a rope. "This is not talking about one in number but one in unity, harmony, peace, and the sharing of common goals."[83] "Echad serves to portray the same range of meaning as 'one' does in English, from the very narrowest sense (one and only one, as in Ecclesiastes 9:18

(one sinner destroys much good) to the broadest sense (one made up of many, as in Genesis 2:24, where a man and his wife 'become one flesh'))."[84] The bride and bridegroom joyfully anticipate becoming one. When we are one with God or another person, we walk in His ways and desire to teach others the path to walk on.

But God's heart is not satisfied with unity between the Father and Yeshua—they want to include us!

We can only begin to grasp the unity between the Father and the Son. They love each other so much that they want to see the other exalted. *"I have glorified You on the earth. I have finished the work which You have given Me to do. **And now, O Father, glorify Me together with Yourself, with the glory which I had with You before the world was"*** (John 17:4–5, emphasis added). But God's heart is not satisfied with unity between the Father and *Yeshua*—they want to include us! Before the foundation of the world, they had a desire to be one with the human race through the bride. They want us to have that same unity with them and each other. Sounds a bit like the first and second greatest commandments!

*"That **they all may be one, as You, Father, are in Me, and I in You**; that they also may **be one in Us**, that the world may believe that You sent Me. And **the glory which You gave Me I have given them, that they may be one just as We are one: I in them, and You in Me**; that they may **be made perfect in one**, and that the world may know that You have sent Me, and have **loved them as You have loved Me. Father**, I desire that they also whom You gave Me may be with Me where I am, **that they may behold My glory which You have given Me**; for You loved Me before the foundation of the world"* (John 17:21–24, emphasis added). Because the Father is in Jesus, and Jesus is in the Father, so we can be one with each other because the Father and Jesus are in us. God has given us His glory so we can be one! It provides the atmosphere to bring true unity. Only in God can we be made perfect. We cannot perfect ourselves in our own strength. Unity with God is tied to knowing that God

loves me as much as He loves Jesus. Wow! When we know this love in the depths of our hearts, we can see the glory, and the glory can be seen in us.

Unity brings the glory, and glory brings the unity!

Beauty Realm

"I will go before you And make the crooked places straight; I will break in pieces the gates of bronze And cut the bars of iron. I will give you the treasures of darkness And hidden riches of secret places, That you may know that I, the LORD, Who call you by your name, Am the God of Israel" (Isaiah 45:2–3, emphasis added).

"Lift up your heads, O you gates! And be lifted up, you everlasting doors! And the King of glory shall come in. Who is this King of glory? The LORD strong and mighty, The LORD mighty in battle. Lift up your heads, O you gates! Lift up, you everlasting doors! And the King of glory shall come in. Who is this King of glory? The LORD of hosts, He is the King of glory" (Psalm 24:7–10, emphasis added).

As we enter into the glory realm, God promises to go ahead of us to do battle. He will straighten out the crooked places in our lives. Where we have been locked out of our inheritance, He will break down the gates and cut down the bars of our prisons. As the King of glory enters the wilderness place, He releases the treasures of darkness and hidden riches of the secret places. It is a promise of revelation. But the greatest revelation is to know (*yada*) the Lord who calls us by name! Part of the call is to receive the release of God's strategies for the next season.

The glory is where the eyes and ears of our hearts are opened to see the Lord revealed in new ways. It is where we see God face to face, like Moses did in the Tent of Meeting. The beauty realm of God is revealed to us. *"One thing I have desired of the LORD, That will I seek: That I may dwell in the house of the LORD All the days of my life, To behold the beauty of the LORD, And to inquire in His temple"* (Psalm 27:4, emphasis added). This was David's heart cry. We don't know whether David had a vision of the throne room as John the Apostle, Ezekiel, or Isaiah did. But even if he didn't, he definitely had an understanding.

Below is Ezekiel's description of the throne room. As you read the description below, try to picture the colors and textures in your mind's eye. Listen to the sounds:

> *The likeness of the firmament above the heads of the living creatures was like the color of an awesome crystal, stretched out over their heads. And under the firmament their wings spread out straight, one toward another. Each one had two which covered one side, and each one had two which covered the other side of the body. When they went, I heard the noise of their wings, like the noise of many waters, like the voice of the Almighty, a tumult like the noise of an army; and when they stood still, they let down their wings. A voice came from above the firmament that was over their heads; whenever they stood, they let down their wings.*
>
> *And above the firmament over their heads was the likeness of a throne, in appearance like a sapphire stone; on the likeness of the throne was a likeness with the appearance of a man high above it. Also from the appearance of His waist and upward I saw, as it were, the color of amber with the appearance of fire all around within it; and from the appearance of His waist and downward I saw, as it were, the appearance of fire with brightness all around. Like the appearance of a rainbow in a cloud on a rainy day, so was the appearance of the brightness all around it. This was the appearance of the likeness of the glory of the LORD.*
>
> *So when I saw it, I fell on my face, and I heard a voice of One speaking.* (Ezekiel 1:22–28)

For Such a Time as This

Transition can be one of the hardest seasons because what seemed like solid ground is now like shifting sand. It is hard to get a foothold. Sometimes the transition of coming out of the wilderness is harder than the wilderness itself. Just when you think you have figured out the "rules" for living, they change again. It is God's test of abundance.

Esther went through a season of preparation that lasted a year. It was a time of being cut off from all distractions and contact with others to focus on preparation and cleansing. For the first six months, she was anointed with myrrh. It is very fragrant, but has a bitter taste. It represents the dealings of God in our lives through sorrow and suffering. Sweet spices were applied to Esther for the second six months. The sweet spices represent her consecration to the will of God. Inner beauty comes from the consecration process. When she went to see the king, she let her attendant (the Holy Spirit) choose what garments she would wear to be presented to the him.

Esther's time of preparation had worked beautiful graces in her. God does not capriciously ask us to endure a season of waiting to merely tantalize us. His timing is part of the process of preparation that does a work of grace in us. Esther obtained favor of all who looked upon her simply because of the beauty of her person. Similarly, it is not our talent, background, inheritance, church, our own goodness nor our Bible training that obtains for us favor of our King. Achievements and works are not items of attraction to Him. Allowing the preparation He prescribes for our lives will create a beauty that satisfies His heart supremely when He looks upon us. Then we will bow at His feet and say, in the words of the old hymn, "Nothing in my hand I bring, Simply to the cross I cling."[85]

"So Esther was taken to King Ahasuerus, into his royal palace, in the tenth month, which is the month of Tebeth, in the seventh year of his reign. **The king loved Esther more than all the other women, and she obtained grace and favor in his sight** *more than all the virgins; so* **he set the royal crown upon her head and made her queen** *instead of Vashti. Then* **the king made a great feast,** *the Feast of Esther, for all his officials and servants; and he proclaimed a holiday in the provinces and* **gave gifts according to the generosity of a king"** (Esther 2:16–18, emphasis added).

Esther's season "in the wilderness" prepared her for a destiny she could not imagine when she was growing up as a Hebrew girl. Who would have thought that one day she would find tremendous favor, become the Queen of Persia, and save her people from mass destruction? *"Yet who knows whether you have come to the kingdom for such a time as this?"* (Esther 4:14). Who would have thought that God is preparing you as a forerunner for such a time as this? This is the time to let God deal with us in the wilderness season so that we can rise up as a voice from the wilderness saying, "Prepare the way of the Lord!" The King of the universe is waiting for His bride who is prepared—You! The body of Christ is transitioning from one realm of glory to another. He will give you the wisdom for the tasks He places before you. It will take courage to transition from the wilderness to your destiny.

Queen Esther waited upon God for the strategy. She had to risk her position and life, to venture out of her comfort zone, to embrace her destiny of saving the Jewish people. She requested the help of family (Mordecai) and her people (the Jews) to fast and pray prior to her stepping into the King's court without being summoned. *"So it was, when the king saw Queen Esther standing in the court, that she found favor in his sight, and the king held out to Esther the golden scepter that was in his hand. Then Esther went near and touched the top of the scepter."* (Esther 5:2). The scepter is a symbol of the power and authority of the Great King. Touching the top of the scepter represents accepting His grace. As a result of taking a risk, the situation was reversed. In fact, Haman's house and property (inheritance) (8:1) and position of authority (8:2) were given to Esther and Mordecai. The king *"gave gifts according to the generosity of a king"* (1:7 and 2:18). Our God is extravagant and can't wait to give of Himself and His treasures to His people. He has much to release to us! His scepter is extended; will you receive from Him?

Ship of Destiny

In the spirit, I was seeing a great clipper ship in the distance. It was beautiful and sparkly, and was moving at a fast pace. As it came closer, I saw the sparkle came from many beautiful gems of all colors covering the sails. The sails were full, although there was no natural wind. The ship sat heavy in the water because it was full of cargo. I knew the ship was full of the destinies of God's people. I asked God what was moving the ship since there was no wind. I then began to see people hiking up the well-worn paths to the high places of God and then coming back down.

It was in receiving heart revelation and understanding in the high places and then learning to walk it out in the valley that the sails were filled to release the destinies. Going up is the first commandment and the coming down is the second. *"Greater love has no one than this, than to lay down one's life for his friends"* (John 15:14).

Now is the time to submit to the process of God to deal with our hearts so we can release His heart. Destiny is released as you walk out what God reveals to you. Now is the kairos time. Don't stop wrestling until your destiny and inheritance are released. Your destiny is to *yada* God face to face, be changed into His likeness, and share this revelation with others. God wants to do exceedingly abundantly above all you can ask or think. Some of us can think big, but it is even bigger!

> *To me, who am less than the least of all the saints, this grace was given, that I should preach among the Gentiles **the unsearchable riches of Christ**, and to make all see what is the fellowship of the mystery, which from the beginning of the ages **has been hidden in God** who created all things through Jesus Christ; to the intent that **now the manifold wisdom of God might be made known by the church to the principalities and powers in the heavenly places**, according to the eternal purpose which He accomplished in Christ Jesus our Lord, in whom **we have boldness and access with confidence through faith** in Him. Therefore I ask that you **do not lose heart at my tribulations for you**, which is your glory.*
>
> *For this reason I bow my knees to the Father of our Lord Jesus Christ, from whom the whole family in heaven and earth is named, that He would grant you, according to the **riches of His glory**, to be **strengthened with might through His Spirit in the inner man**, that Christ may dwell in your hearts through faith; that you, **being rooted***

and grounded in love, may be able to comprehend with all the saints what is the width and length and depth and height—to know the love of Christ which passes knowledge; that you may be filled with all the fullness of God. Now to Him who is able to do exceedingly abundantly above all that we ask or think, according to the power that works in us, to Him be glory in the church by Christ Jesus to all generations, forever and ever. Amen. (Ephesians 3:8–21, emphasis added)

Press into the deep places of God to receive the unsearchable treasures of *Yeshua* so that you can fully receive them into your life by walking them out.

Continue to press into the deep places of God to receive the unsearchable treasures of *Yeshua* so that you can fully receive them into your life by walking them out. Then He will do exceedingly abundantly more than you can ask or think as you let His power work in you to accomplish all He wants.

Anticipation

> " '*Let us be glad and rejoice and give Him glory, for **the marriage of the Lamb has come, and His wife has made herself ready.*' And **to her it was granted to be arrayed in fine linen, clean and bright, for the fine linen is the righteous acts of the saints.*** *Then he said to me, 'Write: **"Blessed are those who are called to the marriage supper** of the Lamb!" ' "* (Revelation 19:7–9, emphasis added).

The destiny of the bride is to be *Yeshua*'s wife, not just His fiancée. It is the time of commitment, not just of being in love. The bride is beautifully adorned in jewels and fine linen. The two best examples of royal weddings are in Psalm 45 and the Song of Solomon. When the voices of the bride and bridegroom are heard, it is an indication of restoration in the Old Testament. There is gladness of heart, music and dancing, and extravagance as seen in John 2:1–11. But most of all, there is anticipation.

Waiting for the Bridegroom

> " '*And **behold, I am coming quickly**, and **My reward is with Me**, to give to every one according to his work. I am the Alpha and the Omega, the Beginning and the End, the First and the Last. I am the Root and the Offspring of David, the Bright and Morning Star.' And **the Spirit and the bride say, 'Come!'** And let him who hears say,*

'Come!' And let him who thirsts come. **Whoever desires,**
let him take the water of life freely" (Revelation
22:12–13, 16–17, emphasis added).

One of the customs in ancient times was that the bridegroom left
the betrothed with family or good friends and went to prepare a
wedding chamber for her. He could be gone up to twelve months.
"In My Father's house are many mansions; if it were not so, I
would have told you. **I go to prepare a place for you.** *And if I go*
and prepare a place for you, **I will come again and receive you to**
Myself*; that where I am, there you may be also. And where I go you*
know, and **the way you know**" (John 14:2–4, emphasis added).
Jesus has gone to prepare a special place for us as we wait for His
return. We know the way.

So what does the bride do during this season of waiting? She
prepares herself, just as Esther prepared for a year before she met
the king. The bride already belonged to her bridegroom when they
became engaged. The first few months she looked longingly at the
tokens of love he left her as bridal gifts, just as we are to be fascinated with the beauty realm of God. But as the waiting time
increased, she was tempted to lose faith and trust that he would
return for her. The consecration to holiness kept her. One of the
symbols of a bride's consecration was a crown. Brides wore a
crown of flowers ("a garden enclosed," Song of Solomon 4:12) or a
golden bridal crown.

We, the bride, are in this season of waiting for His return. As in
many parables, we know neither the time or season when He will
return. I believe it is soon. So we call forth the friends of the bridegroom to prepare the bride in this season. We call forth a bride without spot or wrinkle. Just as God desired in the beginning of time, He
is looking for a bride that is bone of His bones, flesh of His flesh, and
heart of His heart. She must be like Him. She must be conformed to
His character and heart. She must love Him with all of her heart, soul,
mind, and strength. She must be dressed in the beauty of God,
adorned with the pearls and gems that He has given her.

"I will greatly rejoice in the LORD, My soul shall be joyful
in my God; For He has clothed me with the garments of

salvation, He has covered me with the robe of righteousness, As a bridegroom decks himself with ornaments, And
as a bride adorns herself with her jewels" (Isaiah 61:10).

*"Just as Christ also loved the church and gave Himself
for her, that He might sanctify and cleanse her with the
washing of water by the word, that He might present her
to Himself a glorious church, not having spot or wrinkle
or any such thing, but that she should be holy and without
blemish"* (Ephesians 5:25–27).

*"Can a virgin forget her ornaments, Or a bride her
attire?"* (Jeremiah 2:32).

Wedding Banquet

The engraved invitations with gold leaf to the wedding feast have
been extended.

*And Jesus answered and spoke to them again by parables
and said: "The kingdom of heaven is like a certain king
who arranged a marriage for his son, and **sent out his
servants to call those who were invited to the wedding;**
and they were not willing to come. Again, he sent out
other servants, saying, 'Tell those who are invited, "See, I
have prepared my dinner; my oxen and fatted cattle are
killed, and all things are ready. **Come to the wedding."'**
But they made light of it and went their ways, one to his
own farm, another to his business. And the rest seized his
servants, treated them spitefully, and killed them. But
when the king heard about it, he was furious. And he sent
out his armies, destroyed those murderers, and burned up
their city. Then he said to his servants, '**The wedding is
ready, but those who were invited were not worthy.**
Therefore go into the highways, and as many as you find,
invite to the wedding.' So those **servants went out into the
highways and gathered together all whom they found,
both bad and good.** And the wedding hall was filled with
guests. But when the king came in to see the guests, he*

saw a man there who did not have on a wedding garment.
So he said to him, 'Friend, how did you come in here
without a wedding garment?' And he was speechless.
Then the king said to the servants, 'Bind him hand and
foot, take him away, and cast him into outer darkness;
there will be weeping and gnashing of teeth.' 'For many
are called, but few are chosen.'" (Matthew 22:1–14,
emphasis added).

God has sent out the engraved invitations. The wedding garment
is symbolic of God preparing our hearts. Do you want to be one of
the "chosen" ones by choosing to let God deal with your heart?
Remember, the majority of the Israelites opted out of the supper on
the sapphire pavement because they were afraid.

Not everyone who says to Me, "Lord, Lord," shall enter
the kingdom of heaven, but he who does the will of My
Father in heaven. Many will say to Me in that day,
"Lord, Lord, have we not prophesied in Your name, cast
out demons in Your name, and done many wonders in
Your name?" And then I will declare to them, "I never
knew you; depart from Me, you who practice lawless-
ness!" (Matthew 7:21–23, emphasis added).

The God of all the universe is waiting to know (*yada*) you. Will
you let Him in? God is anticipating your answer!

God's Heart Cry

"Come up to the higher realms! Let Me clothe you with humility.
Ask for wisdom and grace. Come into My presence. Ask Me to
remove the veils from your mind so that you may truly see and *yada*
Me as I am, not as the world has perverted your image of Me. Lay
down your burdens of shame and sin and I will cause you to dance
and leap in the high places of My Spirit. Come, come out of hiding
and follow after Me desperately. Ask for more hunger.

"Seek to *yada* My heart with all of your heart. Ask for My love.
Ask for My compassion. Let Me show you My righteous judgment
in your life and in the world. Look for what I do, and listen for what

I say. Follow My lead. Let Me transform you down to the depths of who you are. I invite your passion for Me, to let first things be first. Let Me know who you are down to the core of your being.

I call forth you as My bride. Come up! Come up!

"Walk out what has been revealed to you. Knowledge is nothing without walking it out in your life. Embrace the cross. Follow My lead in the dance of your life. I may ask you to take the road less traveled so that you might find My heart. It may not look like the path to the greatest ministry or influence, but it may lead you closer to Me. I want you to walk in My likeness and in My ways. People will know that you are My disciple because you will reflect who I am. You will be glorious! Come, come, I anticipate your presence in My presence! I love you so much, I ache to have you know My love. I call forth you as My bride. I desire to release My destiny in you. I long to show you My hidden treasures. Come up! Come up!"

Endnotes

[1] *HaYesod* (Littleton, Colo.: First Fruits of Zion, 1999), p. 2.25.

[2] Mike Bickle, *The Pleasures of Loving God* (Lake Mary, Fla.: Charisma House, 2001), p. 51.

[3] By permission. From *Merriam-Webster's Collegiate® Dictionary* at www.Merriam.Webster.com by Merriam-Webster, Incorporated.

[4] Materials from *A Divine Confrontation* by Graham Cooke, copyright 1999 used by permission of Destiny Image Publishers, 167 Walnut Bottom Road, Shippensburg, Pa. 17257, p. 25.

[5] Ibid., p. 135.

[6] Rick Joyner, "Messengers of Power," *The Morning Star Journal* (Charlotte, N.C.: Morning Star Publications, Inc., Volume 11, No. 4, 2001), p. 58.

[7] Richard J. Foster, *Celebration of Discipline* (New York: HarperCollins Publishers, 1978), p. 1.

[8] From *The Divine Romance* by Gene Edwards © 1984m 1992. Used by permission of Tyndale Publishers, Inc. All rights reserved., pp. xi–xii.

[9] Ibid., pp. 32–33.

[10] Ibid., pp. 58–59.

[11] Ibid.,. pp. 176–177.

[12] Ibid.,. pp. 190–191.

[13] David Wilkerson, *The Cross and the Switchblade* (Old Tappan, N.J.: A Chosen Book, 1963), p. 72.

[14] By permission. From *Merriam-Webster's Collegiate® Dictionary* at www.Merriam.Webster.com by Merriam-Webster, Incorporated.

[15] Ibid.

[16] Taken from *Theological Wordbook of the Old Testament* edited by R. Laird Harris, Gleason L. Archer, Jr., Bruce K. Waltke, Moody Press, copyright 1980, no. 848, p. 366.

[17] Ibid., no. 848, pp. 366–7.

[18] Ibid., no. 1879a, p. 752.

[19] Leland Ryken, James C. Wilhoit, Tremper Longman III, editors, *Dictionary of Biblical Imagery* (Downer's Grove, Ill.: Inter-Varsity Press, 1998), p. 390.

[20] Harris, no. 1786a, pp. 728–9.

[21] Notes in the *Spirit-Filled Bible* for Exodus 12:1–11 (USA: Thomas Nelson, Inc., 1996), p. 98.

[22] John Bevere, *Fear of the Lord* (Lake Mary, Fla.: Charisma House, 2000), p. 179.

[23] By permission. From *Merriam-Webster's Collegiate® Dictionary* at www.Merriam.Webster.com by Merriam-Webster, Incorporated.

[24] James Robison, "The Holy Spirit and Restoration," *Spirit Filled Life Bible* (USA: Thomas Nelson, Inc. 1996), p. 2014.

[25] Brian Doerksen, "Refiner's Fire," *Winds of Worship, Volume 3* (Mercy/Vineyard Publishing, 1990). All rights reserved. Used by permission.

[26] Bob Sorge, Tape on "The Wilderness."

[27] Harris, no. 172, p. 76.

[28] Author unknown.

[29] Kay Arthur, *As Silver Refined, Learning to Embrace Life's Disappointments* (Colorado Springs: WaterBrook Press, 1998), p. 4.

[30] By permission. From *Merriam-Webster's Collegiate® Dictionary* at www.Merriam.Webster.com by Merriam-Webster, Incorporated.

[31] Rick Joyner, "Eyes that See," from Word of the Week on the Morning Star Web site (www.eaglestar.org) on February 11, 2002.

[32] Mike Bickle, tape 3, "Cultivating a Heart After God."

[33] Bickle, *Pleasures*, p. 61.

[34] Taken from *The Wycliffe Bible Commentary*, Electronic Database, Moody Press, Copyright (c) 1962.

[35] Nouwen, pp. 79–80.

[36] Bickle, *Pleasures*, p. 17.

[37] Ibid., p. 19.

[38] By permission. From *Merriam-Webster's Collegiate® Dictionary* at www.Merriam.Webster.com by Merriam-Webster, Incorporated.

[39] Ryken, p. 602.

[40] Tamara Winslow, *Common Sense for Confusing Times* (1997 Class Notes), p. 2.

[41] Fuchsia Pickett, *Spirit Led Woman Bible Study: DEBORAH* (Lake Mary, Fla: Charisma House, 1999), pp. 31–32.

[42] Bob Sorge, *Pain, Perplexity, and Promotion* (Greenwood, Mo: Oasis House, 1999), p. 75.

[43] Ibid., pp. 95–96.

[44] Harris, p. 791.

[45] Ibid., p. 291.

[46] Geoffrey W. Bromiley, *Theological Dictionary of the New Testament (Kittel)* (Grand Rapids: Wm. B. Eerdmans, 1985), pp. 389–390.

[47] Sorge, p. 89.

[48] Michael McTwigan, Editor, "Pottery" article rewritten and excerpted from *Compton's Interactive Encyclopedia* (Compton's NewMedia, Inc., 1994, 1995).

[49] Cooke, p. 248.

[50] Bickle, *Pleasures,* p. 8.

[51] Wade Taylor, *The Secret of the Stairs* (Hagerstown, Md.: EBED Publications, 1988,

1993, 1994, 1996, Pinecrest Bible Training Center), pp. 64 and 68.

[52] Henri J.M. Nouwen, *Life of the Beloved, Spiritual Living in a Secular World* (New York: The Crossroad Publishing Company, 1997), pp. 78–79.

[53] Jamie Buckingham, *Where Eagles Soar* (Old Tappan, N.J.: A Chosen Book, 1980), p. 14.

[54] Foster, pp. 1–2.

[55] Max Lucado, *Just Like Jesus* (Nashville: Word Publishing, 1998), p. 82.

[56] Ibid., p. 81.

[57] Robison, p. 2015.

[58] *Intercessory Prayer* by Dutch Sheets, Copyright 1996 (Gospel Light/Regal Books, Ventura, CA 93003. Used by permission, p. 28–29.

[59] Brother Lawerence, *The Practice of the Presence of God* (Old Tappan, N.J.: Spire Books, 1976), pp. 62–63.

[60] Foster, p. 30.

[61] Bickle, *Pleasures*, p. 56.

[62] Foster, p. 48.

[63] Bickle, *Pleasures*, pp. 142–3.

[64] From *A Hunger for God* by John Piper, 1997, p. 93. Used by permission of Crossway Books, a division of Good News publishers, Wheaton, Illinois, 60187, www.crosswaybooks.org).

[65] Ibid., pp. 61 and 64.

[66] Biblesoft's *New Exhaustive Strong's Numbers and Concordance with Expanded Greek-Hebrew Dictionary*, Copyright (c) 1994, Biblesoft and International Bible Translators, Inc.., OT:7725 and NT:3340.

[67] Robison, p. 2015.

[68] Lucado, p. 96.

[69] Buckingham, pp. 131–133.

[70] Cooke, p. 157.

[71] Fred N. Grayson, *Oysters* (New York: Julian Messer, 1976), p. 12.

[72] Anointette L. Matlins, *The Pearl Book, The Definitive Buying Guide* (Woodstock, Vt.: GemStone Press, 1999) p. 4.

[73] Ibid., pp. 63–74.

[74] James Arquitt, "Joseph Ministry in the End Times," *The Morning Star Journal* (Charlotte, N.C.: Morning Star Publications, Inc., volume 11, No. 4, 2001) p. 35.

[75] John G. Lake, *John G. Lake* (Fort Worth, Tex.: Kenneth Copeland Publications, 1994), pp. 48–49.

[76] Ibid., p. xxi.

[77] By permission. From *Merriam-Webster's Collegiate® Dictionary* at www.Merriam.Webster.com by Merriam-Webster, Incorporated.

[78] Rick Joyner, *The Final Quest* (New Kensington, Pa.: Whitaker House, 1996), p. 56. Used by permission of the publisher.

[79] Ibid., p. 118.

[80] From *Hind's Feet in High Places* by Hannah Hurnard, © 1975 by Tyndale House Publishers, Inc. Used by permission, pp. 228–229. All rights reserved.

[81] Joyner, p. 80.

[82] Bickle, *Pleasures*, p. 193.

[83] Dr. Douglas Wheeler, "The Echad of God," *Restore!* Magazine, volume 7, no. 22 (Atlanta: Restoration Foundation, 2002) p. 34.

[84] Word Wealth, *Spirit-Filled Bible* (USA: Thomas Nelson, Inc. 1996), p. 263.

[85] Dr. Fuchsia Pickett, *For Such a Time As This* (Lake Mary, Fla: Charisma House, 1997), p. 56.

Printed in the United States
949000003B